The #1 Enemy of Writing (and How You...)

By Bryan Hutchinson Copyright 2014

www.PositiveWriter.com

All rights reserved. No part of this book may be reproduced or transmitted in any form or by any means, electronic or mechanical, including photocopying, recording, or by any information storage and retrieval system, without written permission from the author, except for the inclusion of brief quotations in a review. Disclaimer: The author is not a therapist or any other type of mental health professional. The author shares steps he's taken to overcome doubt. They are personal experiences, life-lessons and opinion only. This book is intended as food-for-thought. Any similarities to persons or other works are purely coincidental. Do not make any decisions solely based on any ideas, suggestions, advice and opinions contained herein. The author makes no warranties or guarantees. The author shall not be liable for any physical, psychological, emotional, financial, or commercial damages, including, but not limited to, special, incidental, consequential or any other damages. Each reader is responsible for his or her own choices, actions, and results.

Reviews

"If you struggle like I do with self-doubt, then this book has good news for you: you just might be a writer. Like a good friend, Bryan guides you through his own process of facing his inner demons, conquering the craft, and creating work that matters. You won't regret reading it."
—**Jeff Goins**, Author, *The Art of Work*

"With his trademark humility and honesty, Hutchinson has offered another round of encouragement for writers struggling in the trenches. He puts forth a round of solid advice on ditching the negativity that too often surrounds the writing life and moving forward to embrace the blessings of living a creative lifestyle. His thoughts are solid, practical, and always encouraging."

—**K.M. Weiland**, Author, *Structuring Your Novel: Essential Keys for Writing an Outstanding Story*

"One of the greatest barriers I see writers face is unrelenting self-doubt, and this book addresses the issue like I've never seen before. By sharing his own story with signature candor, Bryan reminds us that we're not alone. With insightful and practical advice, he hands over the tools we need to face that doubt, overcome it, and create the work we're meant to create."

—**Dana Sitar**, Author/digital publishing coach, DIY Writing

Read more reviews at:

http://positivewriter.com/writers-doubt-the-book/

Also by Bryan Hutchinson, and Friends:

Special Thanks

Loving thanks to my wife, Joan Faith, for graciously allowing me the countless hours it takes to create, and for reading every word I write. Thanks to my friend Mike Hutcheson, who is always willing to look over what I've written and for not being shy about letting me know when more work needs to be done. Huge thanks to Joe Bunting for his outstanding efforts editing this book and for his kind words in the foreword. Thanks to Jeff Goins and all Tribe Writers members, for your enthusiastic support and allowing me to bounce ideas off of you.

And most importantly, thank *you*.

Contents

Foreword 7

Introduction... 9

You Can Write a Book and Publish It 11

My Story 14

Letting Go 18

The New Market 22

The Key Thing to Remember About Writing 27

Overcoming Your Internal Naysayer 33

Some Cautions to Consider 39

Finding Inspiration and Motivation 51

You Have the Potential 56

Writing is Empowering 61

Writing Rituals 66

The Zone 70

Slaying The Beast 73

Part II – BONUS CHAPTERS on Self-publishing, Blogging and Marketing 85

Publish Anyway 86

Self-Publishing is Easy 91

How to Promote Your Book in Online Communities 97

Why You Need a Blog and to Giveaway Free eBooks........101

Why You Should Dream Big..115

How to become a Professional Author 118

Create Work That Matters 120

Resources 121

Foreword

I was four months into writing my first book when I was struck by what Bryan Hutchinson calls Writer's Doubt. It was my first major job as a writer, and I was already feeling stretched further than I had ever been. Then, one day, I snapped. I remember kneeling on the floor of my home, my manuscript open on the burning hot laptop on the couch beside me. I felt like my whole body was filling up with cold, piercing water. I was drowning. I put my forehead on the floor and moaned. I couldn't do this. I couldn't finish this book. I couldn't be a writer any more. I didn't even want to. I thought about myself five years from that moment and realized I would be happier if I quit being a writer. I never wanted to feel this stupid and helpless again.

That afternoon was one of the best experiences of my life because I learned something that would change how I viewed Writer's Doubt forever. It didn't stop hurting, and I didn't feel better about myself, but I realized how crazy it was that I had my head in my hands and was rocking back and forth on the floor for a bunch of words on a page. This was just writing! It wasn't like I was in physical pain or anything. And so I decided I would finish 500 words. The pain, physical or not, hadn't gone away. Writer's Doubt was still hitting me hard. I still didn't want to be a writer, and I definitely didn't want to be writing that stupid book anymore, but I wrote a sentence, then another sentence. And after an hour and a half, I had 500 words. I took the rest of the night off. And then, in a month, the book was finished.

It's no accident that I completed the book so soon after I experienced the worst case of Writer's Doubt in my life. Writer's Doubt, as Bryan's excellent book shows, is a sign that you're close, that you're about to have a breakthrough. The truth is that if you're on the right track, you're almost certainly going to experience Writer's Doubt. It's normal, it's vicious, and you can't let it stop you.

Since that first book, I've been lucky enough to write several more books, and watch one of them become a #1 Amazon bestseller in the Writing Reference category. I've also gotten to help hundreds of thousands of writers deal with their own fear of failure on my blog thewritepractice.com. And yet, despite experience and success, every time I work on a writing project I care about, I hit a point where I'm convinced I can't do it, that I'll never finish the project, that I'll never be the writer I want to be. This feeling used to debilitate me, but now it excites me. I know that the moment it hits me the hardest, that's the sign I'm about to push through.

I first met Bryan just after we had both been chosen for an award for top writing bloggers. I randomly picked up his memoir and was surprised at how raw and open he was. His writing style was simple, but his story kept me reading far longer than I had intended to. When he asked me to write the Foreword of this book, I knew I couldn't say no.

This book isn't complicated. It won't win a Pulitzer, and it probably won't be reviewed by the New York Times. It's far sneakier than that. I have years of professional writing experience. I didn't expect to be challenged by this book, and then it kicked my butt. Reading it, I realized that I was still holding back. I still wasn't the writer I wanted to be. I thought this was just going to be another writing book. But now I'm a better writer because of it.

I hope you never get to the point where you're kneeling on the floor, moaning, and feeling like you never want to write again. However, if you do and you've read this book, I know even drowning in Writer's Doubt won't stop you because, as Bryan likes to say, "You're a writer!"

—Joe Bunting, Author, *Let's Write a Short Story!*

Introduction

> "If the Sun and Moon should ever doubt, they'd immediately go out." —William Blake

Thank you for your interest in this little book on writing. It's a personal journal, of sorts, that chronicles how I rose above my angst to write every day and publish my work. This is an account of one person's drive, mine, to pursue my passion to write, despite being told by so-called experts that I would never be a writer. This is a book that demonstrates that you don't need to be a master to write books, much less to become a bestselling author.

I started writing my first book in 2007 when I was 37 years old. Since then I have written eight books, over 1000 blog posts, and quite a few magazine and newspaper articles. It has been one heck of a ride. I've experienced obstacles and setbacks for which I had to find creative ways to overcome. There were times when I didn't think my books would catch on, and times when I thought I was writing only for myself, but as time went on the one thing that mattered most, was that I was actually writing *and* publishing. I've never done something so consistently and prolifically in all of my life. It is because I let go. I stood up to the internal and external naysayers and finally began living my dream and following my passion.

Writer's Doubt is written for writers like me who have struggled with self-doubt and may have been told in one way or another that their writing isn't good enough. For writers who have been at the butt end of criticism to the point of giving up, even if that criticism came from within themselves. I'm here to cheer you on by sharing practical strategies on overcoming Writer's Doubt I've learned on my journey and challenging you to create work that matters.

This book is also a call to action to fellow writers to support one another at every level. Writers can be extremely critical of each other, and I want that to stop. We all have the same goal. We should support each other regardless of the level of each other's writing skills, whether we're just starting out, experienced and professional or just writing purely for the joy of it. I've found that in order to truly grow as a writer, it's better to support fellow writers despite their skill level or success. The exchange of useful feedback with positive reinforcement between writers is a win-win situation by improving the skill level and the confidence of both.

You know what it's like to struggle with doubt, and so do I. This book is not about being a perfect writer or the next Twain or Salinger. It's about doing the work, honing your craft and learning about who you are as a writer. Part of that process is overcoming the doubt that will accompany you every step of the way. With determination, the right strategies and support from fellow writers you can prevail over your fear of rejection and overcome the desire to concede defeat when you're told that you will never be a decent enough writer, especially when it's the voice in your head telling you so.

With that said, there will always be those who will try to bring you down, whether it's for the sake of your improvement or to rid the earth of your writing, so always remember:

You *are* a writer!

I hope you find as much enjoyment and satisfaction in the process of writing as I have. No matter what the obstacles are, or what anyone has told you, I sincerely believe you need to write and share your stories.

You Can Write a Book and Publish It

I know there is a story in you, a fascinating one, and one day you may want to share that story with the world. That's good, because we need your story. We can learn from each other's experiences. Thanks to self-publishing and blogging, books about real life experiences, what I call *reality writing,* are all the rage! Your experiences are valuable, and if you share them you may strike a chord with others that motivates them to try something new. We all have important life-lessons that could help others, and with blogging and self-publishing we can share them easier than ever before.

I do not consider myself a master writer, and you don't have to be one either. I am what you might call a self-taught writer. My formal education ended in the middle of tenth grade when my parents pulled me out of school. And yet, my writing is now good enough to reach thousands of people, mostly because I took the time to learn how to write better on my own. In *Writer's Doubt,* I'll share with you how I did it and how I overcame Writer's Doubt to write and publish books that matter.

When I wrote my first book, *One Boy's Struggle: A Memoir,* it was meant to simply be a therapeutic journaling exercise to help me come to terms with the difficulties I endured as a child. I wrote about my life as a young boy struggling with inexplicable behavior that caused me to be severely punished and ridiculed most of my life. Finally, at the age of 28, I sought help. That boy who always struggled so much to learn and to be accepted, with limited education, found his own ways to become successful and happy as an adult. When I finished writing my story, I felt a weight had been lifted from my soul, and I decided to share it with the world with the hope that someone else could benefit from it.

One Boy's Struggle became a memoir competing for recognition among thousands of other memoirs presented to publishers every day. Furthermore, the subject matter that I discuss occupies a very specific niche in an already saturated market. New books within my niche are continuously being published. So, what made my book unique? What made it stand out? Why has it sold so well in a highly competitive market? I have to admit, I don't have a magic formula. But I'll discuss how I write every day to overcome my angst, the steps I have taken to get myself published, and how I spread the word about my books. I'll reference *One Boy's Struggle* throughout this book to provide specific examples.

Over the last several years I've received an overwhelming number of emails with questions about writing and publishing, but, by an incredible margin, the one question that was asked the most was: "How do you overcome your fears and doubts?"

Through the course of this book, I'll do my best to answer that question, and I'll offer you a few tips about blogging, publishing and marketing, too. Because as you know, writing is more than just writing. Writing is also about what we do and the journey we take to share our writing with others.

I love to write. If you love to write, then join me on this journey to overcome Writer's Doubt. And if for some reason you've come to dread writing, perhaps because you have never been able to write a full book or because you never thought you could write well enough to share your work, I hope I can help rekindle your passion for it. You have it within you to finish your book. I know you do. And it has never been easier to share your work than it is now.

Have you ever been told you that you shouldn't write or that you can't? Have you ever failed a writing class and believed you don't have the talent to become a writer because you're not a great speller or a master of grammar? Or do you simply believe that your writing doesn't cut it?

If you have been informed by educators or other critics that you should give up as a writer, you're not alone. No matter how many experts, teachers, editors, or anyone else told you that you can't be a writer, I'm here to tell you as long as you love to write and have the inner desire to express yourself, no one can stop you but yourself.

Experts, teachers, so-called friends, and the harshest critic of them all, me, told me that my writing wasn't good enough. I had terrible grades throughout my years in school to prove it, but I became a writer and published anyway.

Perhaps the critic that's causing you to stall, even if you've already published work, isn't anyone external. Perhaps it's the critic within you. That's okay, too, because *Writer's Doubt* is written to help you overcome doubt and create work that matters, no matter what the cause may be.

It is my desire for you to use this book as an encouraging tool to help you ignite your passion for writing and overcome any doubts you may have. Writing is a magnificent form of self-expression, and you're good enough!

My Story

I first discovered my love for writing in second grade, but perhaps not the way most people might. As it happens, I was falling behind the other students and was placed in a specialized education class for reading and writing. In this remedial class, there were only a handful of students, and we were given individual attention by the teacher to help us improve our reading and writing skills. Before that I rarely paid attention, was always called out for daydreaming, was constantly looking out the window, and often got lost during lessons. By being in a much smaller class that was specifically focused on reading and writing, I was able to learn better and faster.

I blossomed in that class because my teacher was extremely attentive to the way I learned. She was patient, helping me write my letters, then words and eventually complete sentences. She encouraged me at every step, even when I didn't write every word correctly. Her gentle guidance kept me motivated to improve for her and myself. I soon found that I enjoyed learning and could keep up with the process in her class. She seemed so enthralled with my writing that it gave me confidence and feelings of self-worth. She made me believe that I could do something special. Thanks to one teacher's attentiveness and unwavering support, I uncharacteristically maintained my attention to what I was being taught. It was a mixed blessing, though, because as a result of my progress, I was moved back to my regular class the following year.

Although my reading and writing skills improved dramatically in that specialized class, I still had problems with school. When that one-on-one instruction was gone, I would never have a teacher compliment my writing again, in fact, quite the opposite. Isn't it interesting how people, even some teachers, are quick to put down work you've put your heart and soul into without realizing what they are doing to your self-esteem? Tough love works for some, but for me all it did was to drain my enthusiasm and kill my desire to try, especially since I had an unrecognized attention problem and learning disorder. My second grade teacher understood the power of positive reinforcement and attention, and for the sake of children (and adults, too) the world over, I hope other teachers follow her example.

I may be lacking in formal education, but my love for reading and writing never went away. I spent a lot of time as a child alone in my bedroom reading, daydreaming, and writing. It was, quite literally, one boy's struggle.

In my early teens I spent more of my time in other people's fantasy-lands via books—mainly Stephen King, Anne Rice and David Eddings. I loved how Stephen King could take me off to a pet cemetery in the middle of the night or put me into a demon-possessed car named *Christine*. He scared the living heck out of me, but what was so unique to me was that someone's writing could actually transport me someplace where I could vividly see, hear, smell and *feel* what was being described. Similarly, as an impressionable young boy, Anne Rice had me completely convinced that vampires existed! That was the power of writing, and I loved it.

I used to dream of becoming a novelist, telling stories for others to read and taking people to distant lands within their imagination through my words. The thing is I doubted I could ever actually finish writing a book, much less write something others would want to read.

During my teens and early twenties, I often tried. Alas, I could never actually write a complete fictional story, not even for myself, but while I tried, I read book after book about writing to learn how others did it. The good news about the experience of *wanting to*, but not being *able to* write a fictional book is consequently how many books you read about 'how to write' in an effort to learn how to do it. I absorbed books on writing as much as I absorbed fantasy books and that was a major contributing factor in *how* I learned to write on my own.

Sometimes having the unyielding desire to write isn't enough. We also have to figure out *what* we want to write about. I had always wanted to write, but it took me a long time to realize what I wanted to write about. I eventually figured out I wanted to write about *real life*. My writing was more fluid and complete when

I later wrote about my life experiences in my journals. Perhaps I am not a great writer (see, the doubt never really goes away), but I know now that the message we share is more important than what we believe about the quality of our writing. Editors can make writers look "perfect," but it's the message the writer delivers that makes him or her memorable.

That's where a lot of would-be authors get stuck. They have the desire to write, but they don't know what they want to write about. Up until my late twenties, I thought I needed to write about what was popular, what was in the bestseller section of the local bookstore. I tried to write mainstream fiction. I even tried to write a few short stories, but I never actually finished any of them. I would either lose interest or lose confidence and eventually succumb to doubt, believing no one would want to read the stories I was writing. I still have a few of those stories in an old, beat-up notebook in the basement. Maybe I'll finish them someday.

However, non-fiction is where I found myself thriving, vanquishing my doubts and finishing my stories. Each of us must look inside ourselves for the type of stories we want to write about and how we want to tell them, whether they are true or fictional. As the old adage goes, when in doubt write about what you know and, more importantly, what you *feel* about what you know because that will get you started. The moment will come when you realize exactly what you want to write about because you absolutely love writing about it and you can't stop. You'll find yourself driving down the highway when an idea suddenly comes to you and you'll desperately search for a place to pull over just so you can jot down a quick note so you won't forget. That's when you'll know you've found your niche.

Eventually, as an adult, I decided to enroll in a college-level writing class. That attempt at formal education was short-lived because a professor called me out in front of the entire class to tell me how terrible my writing was. She exclaimed loudly and boldly to the class that my punctuation and grammar were absolutely horrendous. She said unequivocally that I would never be a writer. After her declaration I left the class and never returned.

Teachers have tremendous power to build or destroy. I can't tell you how ashamed I was, how small and ridiculous I felt. That professor's words convinced me to give up writing for good, and I did give it up for many years, even the journal writing that I enjoyed doing just for myself.

When I was battling depression in my late twenties, a mentor and friend of mine loaned me a book he thought might help. The book was *The Power of Positive Thinking* by Norman Vincent Peale. It moved me to seek help for my struggles. I entered into professional therapy for depression at the age of 28, and I began to learn how to live a more fulfilling, happier life. I took Peale's teachings and what I learned in therapy and combined them to produce my own unique personal perspective, which became the impetus of *One Boy's Struggle*. I wanted, and still strive, to do for others what Peale's book and therapy did for me. Therapy and Peale's teachings helped me discover what I wanted to write about and I finally left fiction behind for non-fiction. Most importantly: I started writing again!

However, it wasn't like I suddenly decided to write and set out with some sort of perfect plan. I didn't have a plan, and the writing I did was an incidental result of therapy. I did not sit down and decide I was going to become a writer; I merely began to write and the words came forth. The difference is that in the past I had tried to force myself to write something, something that wasn't really begging to come out, but when I let go and wrote what I was inspired to write, the words came forth as if they had been waiting there all along. I had something to write about all the while, poised to be expressed. I did not intend to publish my memoir when I started it. It was during the course of writing my story that I thought my story might help others.

The amazing thing, at least to me, is that when I finally wrote my story I didn't start with any kind of outline. Instead, I wrote straight from the heart and allowed my story to pour forth, and because of that, I was able to ignore the self-doubt that would usually interrupt my thinking. That's how it all started. Without realizing it, I had done the hardest thing. I let go and just wrote.

Letting Go

I have immeasurable respect for my readers. My motto is: respect and admire your readers and they will respect and (hopefully) care about you in return. But remember, not everyone will like you, even some who have never read your work. It's human nature, so never set the impossible goal of trying to please everyone. You can't and you won't. If you try, you risk writing a diluted, half-hearted version of your message so as not to disrupt the status quo. Readers will respect you if you stand your ground and never lose sight of your personal vision, even if your message is controversial.

Many people tell me that *One Boy's Struggle* has taught them more about themselves and what they can do to overcome their struggles than any other book they've read. I don't know for certain why the book touched them as it did, but I am grateful that my story has helped so many. Inspiring writing sometimes happens by accident, but it can only happen when you're brave enough to let go and let yourself write, even if what you're writing doesn't seem to make complete sense at the time. My first book was unplanned, but this is the experience I think most of us want to happen with our writing. We want our writing to flow from us, unencumbered by doubt.

If I had intended to write a memoir I may have been a little more careful in some of the things I revealed, especially about my experiences with my father. Those revelations incited many heated arguments within my family. Understandably, they didn't really appreciate that I shared all of my negative childhood experiences with the world. Families, in general, tend to believe certain things should remain private. However, that's the thing about a life filled with extreme difficulties-if we keep our stories, our feelings and our experiences hidden inside of us, it is much more difficult to heal and find answers. So many people remain secretive, so secretive that they're never able to actually seek help for their internal conflicts. If you want to be honest with your readers and yourself, put everything on the page and leave your comfort zone behind. It's a risk to be sure, but you can always remove what you can't or *shouldn't* publish later. That is entirely up to you. If something is critical about someone living, sometimes you can change descriptive information and names in order to get around legal problems, but the information is imperative to your story. (Note: This isn't legal advice. Consult a legal expert before publishing material that could be inflammatory, offensive, or questionable.)

I mention the above because many people write books with the intention of publishing them from the onset. That's okay, but sometimes the writing process tends to be controlled, so much so that the emotional core of what they're writing rarely makes it to the page. When this happens readers are likely to fail to connect with the writing or the author. I believe my books do well because people can relate to them.

If you're going to write a book about your experiences, even with the intention to publish it, try not to hold back—correction: *don't hold back*. If you try to write perfectly, you may fail to write openly enough to connect with your readers. You can always go back and organize your writing later, or have someone help you do it.

The best thing a writer can do is let go and write. Too many of us spend too much time trying to find the ideal method to get our words on paper and labor over organizing what we want to say. Following an outline* or using state-of-the art writing software works for some people, but if you find yourself in an endless cycle of trying to find that magic formula or perfect system to writing the next bestseller, then my advice is to stop searching and start writing. Let your thoughts form into words on the paper as they come. Don't force them. Allow yourself to step out of your normal routine for a few hours each day and put whatever comes to mind on paper without censoring or organizing it. By doing this you'll have a better chance of bypassing the mental filters of "what I have to say isn't good enough," "this isn't in order," or "this doesn't make any sense." Most of us allow doubt to stop us before we ever get started.

However, it does help to be prepared when you've let go and the ideas start coming. Here are some helpful, basic tools I always keep at the ready:

- Notepad: I always carry a notepad with me. These days, my smart phone serves as my notepad, but a simple pad of paper serves the same purpose. Whenever an interesting idea comes to me I make a note of it. I can't stress how important having a notepad with me at all times has been for me. We process a lot of information each day and come up with a myriad of ideas. Trying to commit it all to memory is impossible. Having a notepad with me at all times helps me remember the ideas that came to me throughout the day. I've written entire articles when I was out shopping or eating lunch using my notepad.

- Digital voice recorder: I use this so that I can take advantage of ideas while I am driving, or when my hand has started to hurt from note taking! Many smart phones have voice recorders, but you can also purchase simple voice recorders at electronic stores.

- Journals: All too often writing is just about getting started. But for me, the hardest part has been simply to sit down and do it. One of my solutions has been to keep a journal. When I lie down to bed at night, I like to write a few things about my day, what I learned or what I experienced. By doing this, I always keep myself writing. It's much harder to fall into writer's block when I am continuously writing. If I take a few days off from writing, it's much harder to start again. As with my notebook, I have written many articles that started in my journals.

- A computer: This is where I put all my writing together from my notebook, journal and voice recorder. My writing desk is in a quiet place surrounded by items that inspire me (in a later section, I'll reveal what those inspiring items are). What's important for you as a writer is to have your "place" where you do your writing daily. The key is to have an isolated, comfortable place that is always used for serious writing. That way, when you arrive there you're more likely to be mentally conditioned to let go and to start writing.

*If you find outlines helpful, consider reading: *Outlining Your Novel: Map Your Way to Success* by K.M. Weiland

The New Market

Writing is subjective. Readers choose what they want to read based on their personal preferences. Until recently, there was a huge gap of writing that had never been available. But because of the revolution in the publishing industry, readers are proving they want to read books that are not handpicked for them. The new readers' market is not always looking for perfectly written books. Instead, readers are often interested in stories they can connect to. For many readers, the presentation of the material has become secondary and, in some cases, irrelevant. Of course, they won't read any book, especially one so filled with mistakes they can't understand the writing, but they won't nitpick books to death that are appealing and enjoyable to read.

We can thank the Internet and thousands of individual bloggers that got up the nerve to write for the masses even though they aren't all writing experts. Actually some bloggers are incredibly difficult to read due to their abundant lack of writing skills, but somehow they still get their meaning across and capture the interest of readers. On the other hand, you may have awe-inspiring writing skills. If amateur writers can become huge, attention grabbing bloggers, imagine what you can do.

It wasn't too long ago that bloggers shocked the world by taking to the Net and sharing their opinions, typically with very simple, basic writing that often had typos in it. More than a few went so far as having a total disregard for any writing standards whatsoever. At first no one really thought this mattered because much of the writing was considered irrelevant. However, *the revolution caught on,* and it initiated a change in publishing no one could have imagined before the Internet. Many newspapers and magazines were totally caught off guard and were very late to the game, but eventually, even they created their own blogs. Even so, most readers still choose to read individual bloggers who are not part of any of the standard media outlets. Many bloggers for media outlets have even been let go over the last few years because they couldn't gain enough of a readership.

What popular bloggers have going for them is their individuality and the ability to relate with their readers in ways that were perhaps not considered, or were considered impossible, before. In many cases, this kind of relatability was blown off as unwanted writing best left to note passing. Some authors and writing enthusiasts even stuck their noses up to "unprofessional" bloggers, but that didn't have any effect on the new readership. Many observers thought for sure that once the professional writers started blogging it would be all over for the "amateurs," but it was too late. The new age for reality writing had come and a revolution of how readers chose what they read and *who* they read began changing faster than anyone could have imagined. And it continues to change. Smart editors for magazines and newspapers now enlist blog writers they never considered before to write on their websites and even publish in their print publications. I happen to be one of them.

Thanks to my blog, certain print magazines have discovered me and have published some of my articles. What's more is that one magazine edited one of my articles so much that I didn't even recognize it. Consequently, it was no surprise to me that the over-edited and deceptively perfect article has been practically forgotten. Another magazine published one of my blog posts with absolutely no editing, and it has been by far my most popular article. This proved to me that while some editors and publishers have a keen understanding for the new market, there are still others that are trying to enforce old standards, which unfortunately may eventually leave them behind in this new age.

Over the last hundred years, most of the books published were so perfectly crafted that only the very best writers (or very famous people) were able to get their writing accepted to be published. As a result we were taught that if we wanted to be a writer then we needed to learn to write as perfectly as possible, and if we couldn't, then we needed to give up the dream. Readers were rarely exposed to imperfection, so there was no way anyone could have foreseen the new readers' market catching on the way it has.

Now, it is exceedingly easy to self-publish at low costs, and many bloggers have discovered they could grow a massive following and have decided to write books. However, they still had difficulty gaining the attention of traditional publishing houses. All this has helped pave the way to the popularity of self-publishing books.

When self-publishing began it was very expensive and not many considered it, but today a person can self-publish a book for the world to buy (if they so choose) for very little or even completely free, such as with Amazon Kindle Direct Publishing. Readers are flocking to self-published books unlike anyone could have predicted before the Internet. Furthermore, some traditional publishing houses are now keeping an eye on popular bloggers and successful self-published authors to the point of offering contracts to those who have proven that their writing sells. Bloggers and self-published authors who may have never before received a publishing contract are now being considered by traditional publishing houses. This isn't only becoming necessary for publishers to stay current, it's smart. For a while it seemed traditional publishers were going to let a new market completely slip through their fingers, even while some may have been struggling to keep the old market stable.

Other industries have also been faced with the same conundrum as publishing houses, unable or unwilling to recognize that new markets have arisen due to the Internet and are here to stay. These new market models are difficult to compete with and are not easily challenged by the old ways. For example, where do most people now get their music? It's not often at a record store. I rest my case.

Clearly, the times for both writers and readers have changed dramatically. If you want to write and you don't consider yourself a professional writer, that doesn't matter. If you create a blog or self-publish a book and readers find you and can relate to your ideas, then a new star could be born. There are now self-published authors who have sold over a million self-published eBooks.

So many stories have gone untold because of the old dictum that you must write as technically perfect as humanly possible and only the publishing house gatekeepers could decide if you were good enough. Don't let your story go untold because of old ideologies. Today, with self-publishing and blogging, you can blaze a new trail with your own form of writing. You can throw the rules out of the window if you want. I don't mean to say you should intentionally write poorly, but if you gain readers with your unique style of writing, even if it's not considered "good" by professional standards, then so be it. It's your prerogative as to how you write. There could be a market of readers out there waiting to read your particular spin on an idea or your creative take, even if it's a subject that is already well written about.

Today, anyone can get a book published, and the public—*the readers*—decide what and who they will read. The thing is, even now, with self-publishing available to the masses, if a book isn't good in some way, doesn't pique the readers' interest, or they can't relate to the information, it won't matter that it *can* be published because people won't spread the word about it. Today it's all about the readers. They choose what they will read, regardless of how it's published or who publishes it. How often do you check which publisher published a book?

However, before rushing off to the presses, consider that today's readers want and deserve a sincere connection with the author more than ever before. If we don't give them that, if we hold ourselves back from giving the readers a connection with us, then it's likely your book, regardless of how it was written or published, won't do well. The good news is that it's easier than ever to build genuine, strong relationships with your readers through your writing, regardless of your writing style and whether you write to meet expert editorial standards.

One type of book you can write to establish a connection with readers is memoir, which is also a terrific fit with self-publishing. A memoir tells your personal story to readers, gives them insights about you that show you are fallible, that you've made mistakes too, and like everyone else, you had to find ways to overcome personal issues. The more you share with readers and give them insight into how you've learned from your trials and errors, the more they get to know you and want to read what you write. That's been my experience. And if you take a good look at social networking and other places where people are connecting online, this is what people are sharing—*their personal experiences*. A memoir can give your readership a back-story about you. If told vulnerably, your story could even be helpful to a great many readers.

If you decide to write your memoir, here are a few tips that helped me:

- Write from your heart because that is where the story is.
- Write for yourself as you want to express *your* story. Try not to worry about whether it makes sense to anyone else or not. Get it on paper first and edit later.
- Try not to think too much about getting it published. Write for the sake of your message first.
- Always have your notebook with you, as memories often come when least expected.
- When I first started writing my memoir I had some difficulty remembering things. If this happens, then start writing what you can remember and memories may resurface during the process, as they did for me.
- Interviews: If you decide to do any interviews remember that no one's memory of you is going to be perfect. Some of the things you remember, they might have forgotten.

If you're writing something as personal as a memoir, it's nearly impossible to follow any specific step-by-step formula without it becoming mechanical. Sometimes, it's best to let it flow, to let the past pour out of you, to write as candidly as you can, revealing the truest part of yourself. Capturing the raw emotion of your experiences is the key to transporting your readers to a place where you've been, and when they can feel, hear, see, and imagine what you have experienced, they are connecting to you.

The Key Thing to Remember About Writing

The key thing to remember about writing: it's about writing! The more we think about it, the harder it gets. We can talk and think ourselves out of writing far easier than allowing ourselves just to write. The mind of a writer is filled with objections because most writers are afraid of writing something that doesn't make sense, or worse, writing something that comes across as idiotic or is considered arbitrary. Your inner voice all too often will put forth resistance, telling you that you don't make any sense whatsoever and you'd be much better off doing anything, except writing!

Maybe you'll recognize some of these inner objections:

Am I really a writer?

Am I any good?

Will anyone care about what I write about?

Does my story make any sense to anyone else?

Do I constantly repeat myself?

Do I over edit?

Do my characters seem real? Do they have depth? Should I just go ahead and kill them all off now and give up writing forever?

Do I suck? No, I don't. Yes, I do.

How bad do I suck? Bad! The Titanic sunk because it knew that I would be born and try to become a writer.

One of the things my inner voice loves to tell me is that my writing is total and complete garbage and beyond any shadow of a doubt will be rejected. My inner voice isn't alone, as so-called experts tried to convince me of the same things, too. Fear of rejection is powerful, because at some point or another we have all been rejected for something, and we never forget the pain. The more times we have been rejected for anything, the more doubt compounds within us. This is an especially complicated issue for writers, because we've all heard the stories and watched the movies where writers get rejected. Some will even tell you that if you want to be a writer then you better get used to being rejected. It's almost as bad as trying to ask someone on a date for the very first time. The possibility of being turned down isn't just extremely high, it's *going* to happen.

Have I made you feel any better about rejection? I didn't think so. The good news is that the power of rejection holds less threat for writers today. You don't need an editor's approval to self-publish and you don't have to send out thousands of letters to be accepted by any agent or publisher if you don't want to. So then, what's to stop you from writing and publishing your writing? Perhaps it's the internal messaging system we all have that tends to tell us that when doing something, *anything*, it must be done in a certain way or it won't be acceptable. Well, that may have been true for a long time, but when it comes to writing and publishing your work, you are now *the-end-all-be-all* if you want to be.

I think we hold onto memories of rejection because we try to avoid putting ourselves in a position of being rejected again, no matter what type of rejection that might be or from whom. Very few of us, if any, are completely free of this internal fear. All of us have our own way of dealing with it; however, to be truly free of the fear of rejection one must come to terms with it. One way I have done that is to write for myself, knowing I can publish whatever I write if I choose to. That doesn't mean I'll sell a million copies or that it will attract a huge readership, but it's still a freedom that gives me room to write. Blogging helps too, because it can be done regularly, in increments, and articles can be published privately first and then, when we're ready, we can publish them publicly. Blogging also takes a while to gain a readership, so our writing is exposed to readers more slowly. As we gain more readers over time, we naturally gain confidence and eventually worry less about being rejected.

At times, if you want to get past the internal resistance of your own mind, you actually have to give in and allow yourself to write whatever you come up with. Even if your writing seems like terrible, useless drivel that no one will want to read, the more you write and get your thoughts on paper, or on the screen, or on your blog, the less power the internal nay saying voice has.

Writing rituals also help, which I'll get to in a moment. Before writing, you might consider looking in the mirror and telling yourself you're going to write the best gibberish that you can come up with, and then challenge yourself to do exactly that! You may find yourself amazed at how much sense your gibberish makes when you read it back.

If you're like me, then you'd like your first draft to be your only draft, but you probably also know that's not what actually happens. Writing a first draft is mostly just getting your thoughts out of your head, but there's a little more to it. A first draft often only makes sense to you, the writer, and it will need to be shaped and formed during the second and, perhaps, third draft. We sometimes heap unnecessary pressure on ourselves to write a perfect first draft. I don't know of any writer that is ever completely satisfied with his or her first draft. I know I never am. It is the action of writing that matters, not necessarily the content itself.

I am willing to bet every writer on God's green earth has been told their first draft is *crap*. Somehow we come to believe it and even tell ourselves this without ever considering the true mental and emotional impact. I refuse to join the chorus. Allow me to share something very important with you and it took me too long to realize it.

Your first draft **is not** crap no matter how far from perfect it might be.

I regret the many first drafts I've thrown away, because I'll never be able to get them back. An idea is wonderful, but an idea written down is heaven. As a draft, it becomes a physical, tangible manifestation you can refer to and build on. However, throwing away an idea, even symbolically, is painful and wasteful. I think all of us have woken from dreams and wished we had written them down, even if just haphazardly, and even if only to remember them later. How many dreams have you forgotten, but somehow the feeling that they were wonderful still stays with you? What if you had written about a dream while it was still fresh in your mind? What if that became your first draft? What would you refer to it as? I somehow doubt you would call it crap.

Think about it a moment, consider how the word *crap* makes you feel (and I am using the "clean" version of the word)? What emotional value does it provide? The first draft matters the most and it deserves proper credit. The belief you're merely writing crap in order to be okay with the fact that it's not "good" only serves to feed your doubts about your writing.

Every book, every article and every blog post starts off as a first draft. A first draft is when you turn an idea into some coherent form, when you've assembled your loose thoughts from notes collected on napkins, scraps of paper, or from your voice recorder. You know how painstaking this process is. Your first draft is perhaps the most important step to completing your project. It's special. No one's ever gotten to the end without the beginning. Crap is the last thing in the world that your first draft is!

I'm writing this because too many have come to believe that when they sit down and write their first draft they aren't doing something crucial to the creative process. I mean, how important can crap be? Don't throw away another seed before it has the opportunity to grow into something beautiful. Don't discard the memory of another glorious dream before it can be realized.

I discovered this the hard way. If I don't think constructively about what I'm writing, I won't make the necessary mental and emotional investment it takes to see my writing through to fruition. Once I figured this out I lowered my risk of falling into depths of Writer's Doubt and became much more prolific. Your state of mind has a huge influence on your confidence and productivity. Today, when I sit down and write my first draft I have the greatest respect for it. It won't be perfect and it certainly won't be polished, but without the first draft I wouldn't have anything!

If you want to feel better about your imperfect draft, then acknowledge it's incomplete and know that you will shape it. It will take time and hard work. It won't always be fun, but if it was just crap who would want to put that kind of effort into it? Not me. What if you stopped calling it crap and started calling it by its true value? Would that change your perspective and increase the emotional value you place in your work?

Let's be honest here, just for a moment, between you and me, in the real world what do you do with crap? I'm thinking of a word that rhymes with plush. You're too good for that and your first draft is, too! No matter how imperfect it might be and no matter how much work must still be done.

With respect and admiration for Ernest Hemingway who said, "The first draft of anything is shit!" I prefer this quote from Michael Lee:

"The first draft reveals the art, revision reveals the artist."

Starting a new writing project is an exciting, mysterious, and sometimes nerve-racking adventure, so try not to limit your process. I have several ways I use to get myself started. One very effective method is talking to myself.

Do you ever talk to yourself? When you're alone (I think you'll really want to be alone for this one) go ahead and start talking to yourself. Talk about anything: how the day has been, why you didn't do something you should have done, a situation at work, or whatever happens to be on your mind.

Here, I'll help you with a couple of questions: What do you

really want to write about? Is there a special story that you want to tell? Talk out loud to yourself about that story, tell yourself openly and honestly why you want to write it. Now here's the key to this exercise—while you're talking, make sure you have a word processor open and type everything that you say, every single word. Don't look at the monitor. No, don't do that! Carry on your conversation with yourself until you've said everything you need to. Try not to hold anything back. When you're finished talking, then, and only then, look at the monitor. There's your first draft ready to be fashioned into your story. It might not be perfect, it might not be exactly what you wanted to write, but it certainly isn't crap. It is a start and it's your very own personal invitation to continue writing.

Like I said, writing is about writing and sometimes it's not what we write, but the actual process of writing that matters the most.

Overcoming Your Internal Naysayer

Over the years, I've worked hard to break the hold of my internal naysayer, and I've written about my efforts with that battle in my books. As much as I've improved, my internal naysayer is still there, even though, thankfully, I've removed much of his power over me. We can never completely rid ourselves of the little imp inside of our minds that tells us we will be rejected, disliked and will pretty much always write worthless drivel. But we can lessen his impact and relegate him to a corner where he can do the least amount of harm. Otherwise, he will rage out of control, inhibiting us from doing the things we want to do, live the way we want to live and writing what we want to write.

A writer who is inhibited and overcome with doubt cannot tell her story. There are many situations in life where one must be restrained, cordial and all that kind of stuff, but there are times to let go, times to dance, times to take off the chains and let loose. We're all inhibited in certain areas of our lives for our own reasons. To be a good writer, an honest writer, *and a writer who actually writes*, it's important to reevaluate one's inhibitions. If writing about certain situations disturbs you or makes you cringe, then by all means write about them. Because our internal demons have a voice, too, and it might pay off to listen to what they are trying to say. Sometimes we have fears that have no relevance in our lives anymore, but because we've never actually faced them, they are still in our heads filling us with uncertainty. We've become so used to the disapproval that we haven't taken the opportunity to write about it, understand it, and, challenge it. Even if our fears are long since irrelevant, they can still stop us from writing and accomplishing our life goals.

You may even discover that your inner demon (if that's what you call it) is not a demon after all. My therapist explained to me that my younger self was still inside of me begging to be heard. He calls it "my inner child" and, from what I understand, we all have one. As I understand it, our inner child holds onto fears, confusions and misunderstandings from our childhoods When we write about the things that make us cringe, we allow the child to tell us his or her story, which is really our own story. Only when we discover the child's story can we start to tell ourselves that those fears no longer need apply to our lives. Of course, this isn't meant to be a therapy lesson, so please don't take it that way.

In my experience, inhibitions about writing in one area of your life leads to inhibitions in other areas of your writing, and readers notice it. When you allow yourself the freedom to write about something that you normally would reject you're opening the doors to new ideas, new possibilities and letting go. But, remember, just because you write about something does not mean you have to publish it. File it somewhere where no one will find it (I don't recommend throwing away any of your writing).

If you want to break your writing inhibitions, write about your fears and what your internal voice is saying. This puts the naysayer in his (or her) place. Sometimes, when you break doubt's power over you in one area of your life, you can also break free from other restraints you didn't realize were there. The more I let my fears rule me, the more they grew and stunted my writing. When inhibitions overwhelm you, they also control you. Then, whenever your inhibitions are challenged, it causes you to fight back, to get angry, and to hide what you genuinely want to say. You have to persevere, to write anyway in order to break free from your inhibitions and insecurities. Fortunately, there is one thing I can guarantee—your computer won't reject you or shut down on you for writing whatever you write. Well, I hope not.

Here's another way to keep your doubts in check. If you were ever to visit me in my home and see my writing desk, you would discover dozens of short statements of affirmation, many of which would be attached to my computer monitor. Statements such as:

- "I am a writer!"
- "I write with passion!"
- "I am having an impact!"

- "I am making a difference!"
- "I always have something to write about!"
- "I am not the reason the Titanic sunk!"
- "Yes, I can write!"
- From readers: "Thank you for sharing your story!"

These statements help me prevail during those times when doubt is playing havoc with my thoughts. There's nothing wrong with having a few statements that motivate, inspire and remind you that you're writing something worthwhile. If you've ever been given a compliment on your writing that really meant a lot to you, how about writing it down and placing it somewhere you can readily see it? As I write this, I have some of these looking at me right now. On my wall, I also have a few magazine articles that encourage me. All of these things help me write, even when my internal naysayer is telling me I suck.

I know firsthand how hard it is to overcome your writing inhibitions. But once you do overcome them, or at least move in the direction of overcoming them, you may find an oasis of useful material. You can even laugh in your naysayer's proverbial face if he provides you with the material you actually use in your writing. We all have fears and doubts. Your fears can even turn into your motivation for writing. In other words, your fears can control you or you can control them. You can turn the tables on your fears and doubts and use them for the good of your writing. This might not happen overnight, but when it does happen, you may find an everlasting fountain of authentic writing within you that never stops flowing.

What I write here comes from my experience, the *been-there-done-that* kind. When I was writing my life story I had to tell the truth of my childhood, and I did not want to revisit those memories. It was too painful, and I did not want to go there, even without the intention of publishing it. Inhibitions can cause you to reject your writing without any real thought as to why you're doing it. Inhibitions can even lead you to animosity and overpowering guardedness.

When I finally broke down, let go, and wrote what I needed to without holding myself back, I started to uncover memories I had long since forgotten. Had I not broken free from my chains of inhibition, I would have never discovered and written about these memories. In the process I learned about myself and how far I have come, and as a result I have a greater respect for what I did to get here. Now, it's clear why my therapist suggested I take on the exercise of writing my story. It was to discover the things that I was scared of, that I didn't want to remember, to remove my subconsciously imposed protections and release fears that no longer apply to my life. *Note: If you have PTSD, or have survived a traumatic past, please don't attempt to rid yourself of past demons by "writing them out" without first discussing it with a therapist.*

Few words make us react the way the word "inhibited" does, but that's also because few things in life make us "act" in certain ways than personal inhibitions do. Although restraint and discretion are necessary in daily life, when it's time to write, those same qualities can paralyze our creative process. As writers we must try to allow ourselves to write about anything that comes to mind, to free ourselves from any self-restraint that could be blocking our story. It's up to you how far you go, and again, I stress that you shouldn't publish *everything* you write. Uninhibited writing is excellent for a personal journal.

When our doubt rages out of control, we have difficulty finding the motivation to write. Another way to quiet our naysayer is to discover what best motivates us to write. We regulate our fears by focusing on something more powerful and positive. Some of us don't allow ourselves to refocus because our internal voice of doubt is so loud we can't ignore it. Try to visualize that negative voice, picture him in a funny clown suit hopping up and down with a silly rattle, and then imagine he has a big mute button on his chest. Now press that mute button and focus on what makes you smile and laugh. Take notice of something beautiful. Allow other wonderful things to eclipse your negative thoughts for a while and write.

But what if you sincerely don't consider yourself a good enough writer? Nearly all the writers I know, at least from time to time, think that their writing is riddled with mistakes and useless information, even their published work. Sometimes I won't read something I've published, because if I do, I will find too many things I could have improved. This becomes more obvious as we grow as writers. Instead of being upset with your writing flaws, allow yourself to see those flaws as markers of your improvement as a writer, effectively turning them into positives.

No matter what we do or how far we've come, we may never be completely pleased with what we have written. That's normal, and sometimes even helpful, because it can serve as an alert. For example, when I think I have written something especially masterful, that's usually when I have been over indulgent and maybe a little intoxicated with my own words. If you get the feeling that what you have written is absolutely perfect, then do yourself the favor of letting it sit a few days to let your emotions about it settle. Once you've allowed the euphoria to wear off a bit, then go back and read the piece and see if you still feel the same way. If you're not sure about it, then perhaps share it with a trusted friend or two and see what they think.

Writing is about taking a risk, a leap of faith, if you will. Consider jumping into a lake without testing the temperature of the water with your toes first. That's often what writing is like; we never know exactly what the temperature is, even if we have taken a dip in the lake before. Writing is so subjective you could write something one reader will absolutely hate and several more will absolutely love. You have no way of knowing beforehand either way. The best thing to do is to continue anyway. We have all been told that life is not without risks. If we don't take a risk or two we will never do anything great with our lives, but the confusing part is realizing what a worthy risk is. A worthy risk is to put down anything you're thinking. Another risk is standing up to your internal fears and writing about them. The biggest risk of all, for many of us, is, after having been told you're not a good enough writer, then setting out to prove to yourself that you'll write anyway.

Sometimes, I think it's good to feel a little worried that what we have written won't be completely understood or accepted. This way we can become more aware of what we're writing and why we're writing it, which helps us put our words to paper with some forethought. The problem arises when those same worries stop us from letting go. Instead, focus on content, style, and audience in your second and third drafts. In your first, take risks. The more often you do, the more you will come to realize that your writing is good enough.

I bet you can remember someone in your life, a teacher perhaps, who picked your writing apart to the point that you felt so small you were willing to give up and never write again. Write about that person's words, chronicle every detail of how you felt from that experience. Then for the very last sentence, after you have finished, add this:

I am going to write anyway!

Writing enables us to free our minds, to move beyond the past, and if we decide to share our writing, we may inspire others to overcome their doubts and find their way as well.

Some Cautions to Consider

Obviously, many things can block us or cause us to doubt ourselves to the point that we stop writing, but some of those things are so common and seemingly harmless we don't realize their impact until it's too late.

To be concise or not.

I've read numerous times that we need to write less to say more, that we should use fewer words to make our point more quickly, and I fell for that dictum and caused myself to stall. It's because I didn't understand the secret to being concise. By writing our initial drafts too concisely we can inhibit our ability to let go and write freely. Limiting your words for the sake of being concise can cause you to doubt what you truly want to write.

Most of us need to use more words to communicate our ideas in our own particular style. Certainly, we're all guilty of being too verbose at one time or another, but consider this: A higher price is paid when you use too few words and don't say what you mean to say, or when you use the wrong words because you're looking for a shortcut. Only you can find the right balance. I do believe that an over commitment to conciseness stalls a lot of writers. It personally caused me to inhibit my natural writing. If trying to write concisely takes away your enthusiasm or makes you too self-conscious, then don't do it. Write freely. The secret to being concise is in the rewriting and editing process, not in the first draft.

Everyone has an opinion.

One of the mistakes I made when I initially considered publishing my first book was asking too many people for their opinions about my writing. Everyone had an opinion, and I easily became overwhelmed. From this mistake, I learned there were a couple people who were consistently helpful with their advice and opinions. One of those people is my wonderful wife, who truly cares about my writing. I hold her opinion in the highest regard and am more than willing to listen to her.

If you're writing a book and let all your friends know about it, you may meet resistance. When you write a book, there are a host of perceptions, for example that you're an expert, that you're intelligent, that you can complete something important to you and many other positive perceptions. It can feel great to tell people you're writing a book! But there can also be a downside. You may create animosity in those who feel you're trying to be better than them or that you will become conceited (or already are!). You deserve to feel proud that you're writing. No one should try to take that away from you, but it's difficult to assure friends and peers that you will remain who you have always been and that you won't become self-righteous.

You may also come across jealousy. Sometimes in life you gain friends because they are similar to you, probably at the same social level. When you publish a book, it may create the perception that you're rising to a new level and those friends may feel left behind and try to stop you. Be aware of this so that you can better discern the difference between genuine, helpful advice and feedback given for the wrong reasons. You don't want people to only tell you what you want to hear. Instead, you want people to look at your work objectively and honestly, to provide you with relevant insight and constructive feedback.

I learned the hard way that it's best to keep knowledge of my writing endeavors pared down to the minimum number of people I've found I can trust. Yes, even as a blogger I sometimes keep other writing projects under wraps until I'm close to finishing. I know this seems like it could delay advanced marketing of a forthcoming book, but sometimes I need discretion to allow myself the freedom to write without any outside influences.

Another cautionary tale: be very careful with sharing your work with a writing class. I say this because you will receive so many critiques that you may get stuck. Remember, critique is what writing classes are all about. If you took the first draft of any bestselling book to a writing class, it would be critiqued as feverishly as any other work, especially if your classmates are unfamiliar with the book or its author.

You have to be very careful when you seek approval from fellow writers. You don't need their approval, and you don't need their criticism either. Why do I say this? The people you need to connect with your book aren't other writers but your intended readers. Writers look at books differently than readers. *One Boy's Struggle* has gone on to become a bestseller and has helped thousands of people around the world, even received public praise from the most notable professionals in its niche. Dissertations have been written on it and one therapist even based a guidebook on it. However, if you go to its page on Amazon you'll find critical reviews from fellow writers. When you read their reviews, you discover for the most part it is *the writing* they are reviewing and *not the story*. That's what too many of us writers do. It's in our nature. On the other hand, if you read the reviews from the intended readers *who are not writers,* you'll discover very few of them even noticed any writing issues at all.

Seeking validation, and even assistance, from other writers is a good way to get stuck. If you need help, stick with the one or two people you trust, or hire a coach and good editor. *One Boy's Struggle* could have used better editing, but thankfully the story connected with readers.

I realize what I've said may come across as if I'm upset with past criticism. Well, I am. But that's not why I've brought it up. As writers it's very difficult for us to not comment on other people's writing. After all, writing is what we do, and we follow accepted standards we'd like to ensure others are following as well. I brought it up because critique from fellow writers is all too often ruthless and it helps to understand where such criticism often comes from.

But what if there's something else at work? What if Writer's Doubt influences us when reading other peoples work? *If* you chronically feel the need to *ruthlessly* give your opinion about another writer's work it's probably not about their writing after all. It could be your doubt taking over. Nobody is perfect and doubt can make us feel the need to frown upon anything that seems less than ideal. You may believe you're harsh because you can't shut off your automatic internal editor, but think about it, just because we feel the need to give feedback about a typo or other errors, doesn't mean we have to deliver it in an insensitive manner, does it?

And if our feedback isn't requested, then why do we feel the urge to give it anyway? When we're having a particularly difficult day with our *own* doubt, we may project it on to others. On those days we can be incredibly unsympathetic even if we don't mean to be. Sometimes, we don't realize it at all, and it's not until someone says something to us that we pay any attention to how we gave the feedback.

Unfortunately for you and me, writers deal with doubt more often than almost anyone else. In order to write what matters, we must first conquer doubt not only about whether we're any good but also if anyone will give a damn about what we're writing. Every day when we sit down in front of our keyboards we must conquer or at least subdue our fears just so we can do what we love. Some days we win the battle, but other days we lose and end up merely staring at the screen frustrated and disillusioned. It's those *other days* that we have to watch out for because worse than staring at a blank screen is reading and commenting on work from other people when we are in such a discouraged mood, overwhelmed with doubt.

We can tell doubt has taken over when we start projecting our negative, self-defeating thoughts on other people's writing. We can't help it. Doubt can lead us over a proverbial cliff. And who wants to jump alone? Writer's Doubt messes with our minds in ways that are as deceptive as they are insidious. This is why it's difficult to ask a group of fellow writers for feedback, because we don't know how much their own doubts about their writing is influencing what they tell us.

So what can you do about it? The first step is to come to terms with doubt. It's real and you're going to battle with it every day for the rest of your writing life. You can overcome it; you're going to have to overcome it again and again. And you will! That's why you're reading this book.

You are not alone. We all have doubt to deal with and we all have days when we're ravaged and defeated by it. Unfortunately, doubt can make us want to lash out to share the pain. You might not realize this, but I am certain if you consider it for a moment you'll remember when you've done it. We all have. Doubt can cause us to be rash, unsympathetic and outright mean towards others. The solution is to always be intentionally kind with our feedback. Don't call it criticism. Feedback is a kinder, gentler word, and it's far more effective in helping another person improve his or her writing. The next time you offer someone feedback, consider how you would want to receive it, *and then give it that way*. Start with something positive, what you thought was particularly good. Then talk about what the author can improve and what mistakes need to be corrected. The key is that you want to give beneficial comments and at the same time encourage the writer to continue writing. Don't make the mistake in thinking you're coddling. That would be your own doubt talking. If you think, "How is she going to improve if I'm so nice?" that's doubt talking.

The kinder and more helpful you are to other writers, the less influence your own doubt will have over you. **How we treat others is a reflection of how we treat ourselves.** The more you intentionally control the tone and quality of the feedback you give, the more you will overcome your own Writer's Doubt. Doubt does not want you to be kind and helpful because then its power becomes diminished. Over time, as you become a master of giving feedback that's sensitive to another person's doubt, you will become the master over your own. If you want to know the secret to becoming a prolific writer who is widely read and respected, this is as close to it as you'll get.

What can you do if you receive harsh or insulting critique? By harsh, I mean obvious and direct opinionated comments about your writing ability or style and the not-so-obviously harsh or indirect comments that include passive-aggressive phrases such as, "no self-respecting writer..." or "any real writer..." that undercut you as a writer. When feedback is overtly negative or worse, is insulting, the person giving it loses his credibility. So, you can read it, take it all in like the punch in the gut that it is and then try to discern something helpful from it or ignore it. But don't respond to it, let it be, for it is more about the person giving it than about your work. You need to know that emotionally charged feedback is never about you. It's about the other person. This doesn't mean you haven't made any mistakes or that you shouldn't find nuggets of helpful information. But try not to argue with the critic. It will just cause you to doubt your writing even more. If it seems like someone is trying to hurt you with their feedback, then it's best to move on and find someone else to help. Feedback given with grace is more beneficial to your writing than judgmental and opinionated criticism ever can be. We're more inclined to use feedback given with care than so-called brutally honest feedback.

Alas, who is your most brutal critic? Here's the clincher: **You are**. No one can be harder on you than you! It doesn't need to be that way, though. You can be honest with yourself without being brutal. Too many of us have been taught that blunt honesty is what we need to improve, but this advice has turned into license to inflict coldhearted criticism and then say it's for the sake of the writer. It's not. It never has been. It's for doubt's sake. Doubt is a manipulating trickster. You need to know that what you're doing is worthwhile. You need encouragement to continue growing in your writing. You can't, *and won't*, become a better writer if you don't believe it's worthwhile and if you're not encouraged to do so. Don't beat yourself over the head with a sledgehammer to improve. It doesn't work. All it does is feed your doubt exactly what it wants, creating the vicious cycle of never believing you're good enough. You are good enough. You are a writer!

Let's treat each other with kindness and help each other become better writers. We'd all be better off coaching one another and not tearing each other's work apart. You're probably not like that, but I'm sure you know plenty of people who are. Thankfully, I have been part of some fantastic writing groups, like Tribe Writers and Story Cartel, where the members keep each other motivated, are sincerely helpful and offer one another thoughtful writing advice. If you can find a group like those (or join them), then you're in for a treat. (If you like, visit www.PositiveWriter.com, the resources page to find out more about Tribe Writers and Story Cartel. I also conducted interviews with both of the founders.)

Don't let negative feedback stop you.

"Negative Feedback" strikes dread in writers the world over. It is our proverbial "Boo!" Most of us crave feedback. We want to know our work matters to someone other than ourselves. And yet, too many of us share our work at the wrong time and with the wrong people, which tends to bring forth the words we dread the most, such as "Your work sucks, I hate it—get a day job!" A little extreme, but you've probably experienced something similar. It doesn't matter what you write about, there will be people who absolutely hate it and people who absolutely love it. There will be people who get it, people who don't and people somewhere in the middle. Feedback can help us improve and become better writers, but as I noted it can also put us in a dark hole where doubt grows unabated, a place from which our writing may never return.

I want you to imagine the worst thing someone could possibly say about your writing. Go ahead—don't hold back (unfortunately, this will probably be easy). Got it? Now increase the volume in your head. Imagine the person screaming out his or her hatred at you. Did you survive the onslaught? Good. Now think about it this way: If someone is willing to go to such lengths to get you to listen to his rant you must be on to something worthwhile. If you weren't, then why would anyone make such a ruckus over it?

Each person who reads your work will have an opinion based on his or her wants, needs, desires, interests, experiences, and, of course, the level of doubt influencing his or her worldview. If you create something original and different you automatically increase the likelihood of receiving negative feedback. This is normal. In general, most people accept things the way they are and reflexively show strong resistance when an idea demonstrates possible change to the status quo.

You can also get negative feedback if you're a previous unknown who comes out of nowhere getting a crazy amount of attention. Jealousy runs rampant when someone seems to skip the normal, accepted steps it takes to get noticed. This is one of the reasons self-publishing has been frowned upon. This might not apply to you today, but be forewarned because if you're creating art and sharing it online, then it could happen tomorrow.

Why did the self-published song "Friday" by Rebecca Black become such an international viral hit if so many people claimed to hate it because it was so terrible? Simon Cowell who wisely advised Rebecca not to "listen to anyone over the age of 18" called it "Brilliant!" It has over 167 Million views on YouTube as I write this, and no one liked it? Who's fooling who? If you were a singer who caught the attention of a producer as successful as Simon Cowell would you believe you created something worthwhile? What if your self-published book was downloaded millions of times and Stephen King called it "Brilliant!" but thousands of people who haven't taken the same risk as you called it terrible? Who are you going to listen to?

We do need feedback to grow as artists, but the key is to ask for feedback from the right people when you're ready, not during the process. What do you think would have happened if Rebecca had received such feverish criticism while she was recording "Friday"? Neither you, I, nor Simon Cowell would have ever heard of her. If you were Rebecca Black would you listen to Simon Cowell, who has sold more than 300 million albums for artists, or to the "haters" who were probably more filled with jealously than anything else?

Here are a few tips for helpful feedback:

- Only ask for feedback when your work is ready. Feedback, regardless of what kind, can influence your creative process.

- Ask the right people. If you ask someone who is resistant to what you're presenting, then you will increase your chances for negative, unhelpful and counterproductive feedback.

- Choose only a couple readers who you respect, who are qualified and open to the type of ideas you have. They should be honest and willing to give you feedback that might not necessarily be what you want to hear, but have the goal of helping you shape your work into something great.

- Ask for specifics and clear examples. Vague statements are unhelpful and can leave you lost as to what to do next.

- It's your work, so make the changes you feel comfortable with, and then let go.

Once your masterpiece is ready to be shared with the world, it's time to come to terms with the reality that you will receive a variety of feedback, not all of it constructive, positive or relevant. Keep moving forward. The good news is, you and I, we're always learning, improving and growing as writers. We're not perfect and that's okay. Just don't let negative feedback stop you. Your writing matters.

Honesty is dangerous

The dangerous part of writing and sharing our stories isn't always the writing itself or even the story. It's more about how it may affect others, and how they might react to it. Honesty is always dangerous. People react to honesty in various ways depending on where they are in their lives and what their experiences and worldviews may be. You can't control how others view things, and you shouldn't try to, but perhaps more importantly:

Don't let others stop you from telling your story.

Everyone interprets things differently. And, unfortunately, this stops too many of us from telling our stories and honestly writing about what we believe. When I wrote my first book about growing up I knew I was voicing issues that others might want to keep secret, issues that even to a degree were blamed on me—hey, I even blamed myself. It was painful to write. Shame that had plagued me for years was pouring onto the page, but I wrote anyway. I learned that you need to tell your story, even if it's just for you.

I had other concerns when I finally decided to publish. I knew some would call me names, tell me the story is a ranting pity party, and some would threaten me with physical harm, even sending death threats. And yet, I published it. Did my fears come true? Unfortunately, yes, some of them did. And that's important to acknowledge, because too often we're told not to worry, most of your fears are just your imagination going wild. Even though some of your fears might seem a little irrational, you still have to come to terms and accept them. We'd like to believe everyone will support and encourage us, but, again, there are those who will tear you down and try to hurt you.

Perhaps you fear one-star reviews on Amazon? There's nothing wrong with your work not resonating with some people. The problem comes when you try to appease those few and change your writing.

Here's a quote to consider from Seth Godin about one-star reviews:

> "I've never once met an author who said, *'Well, my writing wasn't resonating, but then I read all the 1-star reviews on Amazon, took their criticism to heart and now I'm doing great'*..."

The reality is harsh criticism most often comes from those who have never put themselves out there. Maybe doubt is holding them back. It's always easier for someone who has never taken the risk themselves to tell you what you're doing wrong or what you should have said. That doesn't mean all input about your work will be unhelpful, but harsh criticism doesn't come from people concerned about being helpful. Of course, you should ensure you're respectful and lawful, but doing so doesn't make it any easier to take criticism. I took a leap of faith writing and publishing *One Boy's Struggle*, and even though some of my fears came true, my memoir has gone on to help thousands because it's a story that needed to be told.

The message in my story mattered so much that one of the most well known professional's in my niche said this about it:

"It's a real eye-opener! Bryan writes of hope and despair, and the all-too-common conflict between desperately wanting to achieve and please, yet suspecting that you'll fail again… and soon." —Dr. Edward Hallowell, bestselling author of *Driven to Distraction*

What I want to emphasize is that if we hold our stories inside of ourselves due to our doubts, we miss the opportunities telling our story may provide, such as saying what needs to be said, helping others, reaching people you never thought you could reach, and the knowledge that what you're writing is important—important if for no one other than you.

When I wrote another book, *Happy Every Day: Simple, Effective Ways to Better Days* I took the leap again. Writing *Happy Every Day* was not nearly as dangerous as writing *One Boy's Struggle*. There were two main differences: I knew I would publish it before I wrote it, and I wasn't revealing details about my life and my past. I didn't want to rewrite my memoir because that would be too painful. Instead, I wanted to take the lessons I learned throughout my life and break them down into the simplest, easiest strategies as possible for creating happiness in one's life on a daily basis.

If the book you want doesn't exist, then write it.

The lessons of happiness were extremely difficult for me to learn, mainly because of my inherent stubbornness and impatience. I read a great many books about happiness (more than I care to admit), and the problem for me was that they spent too much time explaining what happiness is, and the processes outlined for achieving it were overcomplicated. The books I read were good books and helped in the long run. However, I wanted to read a book that took a simpler approach, and that's one of the reasons why I wrote *Happy Every Day*.

Writing about happiness you might think seems harmless, but it's not. *Happy Every Day* comes from my own life lessons, which opens it up to disagreements, and since happiness is highly subjective, I knew I would touch nerves. I also included suggestions on how to deal with bullies and negative influencers, since I have been on the receiving end of them all my life. Bullies and negative influencers who read the book may well recognize themselves within my words, even though that was not my intention. I'd love to think they would change from reading it, but lashing out is more their style, otherwise they wouldn't be bullies in the first place. Still, I believe being happy is possible even for negative influencers, and if they want to call me names, then it's a risk I needed to take.

Then, there are the people who believe being happy simply isn't possible, and they challenge the book by calling the ideas unachievable or even outright wrong. And you know what? That's okay, because I believe those who challenge the strategies may also try some of them, and who knows, wouldn't it be great if they find a few that work for them? It is never my intention to write anything controversial, but when you're honest, controversy is often a byproduct. *Happy Every Day* simply provides strategies that I believe can help people find happiness in the common every day things and situations we all too often overlook. Was it worth the risk? That's a fair question, but it's a question that needs to be answered *before* writing. The answer was and is, YES! For those who like to measure results, to date, *Happy Every Day* has over 100 reviews on Amazon.

When you tell your story honestly, even if only to share the lessons you've learned, it's dangerous because it's personal. Each person will read into it based on their own experiences and beliefs. It's important to know that just because some people disagree with you, it doesn't necessarily mean they are right or wrong, just that they see things differently. Their opinions are just as valid in their own right as yours or mine. If you want to write your story honestly, you'll come to a point where you have to make a decision about whether you're going to take the risk of being honest, because no matter how harmless it seems to you, you will write something dangerous. My suggestion: Write it anyway. That's what writers do. The thing to come to terms with is: Are you going to allow others to stop you? As you know, sometimes, the "others" is really ourselves.

Finding Inspiration and Motivation

One place many novice writers, and even published writers, find themselves from time to time is in the chasm of writer's block. Uninspired and unmotivated, it's a scary, cold and very dark place. None of us like being there long. What we need is inspiration to compel us to write. Luckily, there is an abundant amount of thought-provoking stimulation available around us every day. I'll give you some of my own personal examples and maybe they will trigger some for you.

For the longest time, I used to wait for something to excite and compel me, without taking direct action to create those things for myself. I think a lot of us tend to fall into this unfortunate trap, but when we wait around passively, we tend to wait a very long time. Sometimes reading positive affirmations is enough to get my writing flowing. But there are many other things that can induce me to start writing. I used to be blind to many of them. I expect that when I present a few, some of these inspiration generators will seem obvious, while others may surprise you. However, as obvious as these inducements may be, a lot of us ignore even the most obvious.

When I was a child, I used to absolutely and irreverently hate going to museums, especially art museums. They were boring, the art always looked weird, and none of it seemed to have any specific purpose. Then I met my wife, Joan, whose family is devoted to art, especially paintings. When I started visiting museums with Joan it took me a while to get into it. The visits remained quite boring until I started to take interest in the artists who created the paintings. It was when I read an enlightening description hanging on the wall next to one particular painting that I suddenly realized something profound: many artists, such as Vincent van Gogh, Rembrandt and writer, Emily Dickinson, whose work we have come to know and appreciate were not well-known, well received, or in some cases, not even recognized during their lifetimes. Doesn't that seem odd? It did to me, but learning this helped me realize something. It was a watershed moment. Despite the lack of validation from others, these artists created work that matters anyway.

The stories of these artists changed everything for me. Many artists broke every rule concerning their art during their time. They created new, radical art styles, and even though they were rejected, they kept making groundbreaking art anyway. So many artists who we praise today were people who took matters into their own hands, essentially "self-publishing" work in their own unique style whether they would be noticed or not. Now, of course, we call their art classics.

Revolutionaries are often mocked until they change everything for everyone who comes after them. If you ever think things won't change and that the standards today will be the standards of tomorrow, you only need to look to the history of artists such as, Leonardo da Vinci, Michelangelo and Picasso, to understand that nothing could be further from the truth.

I often write about creativity, how I believe it's inherent in all of us and doesn't always need specific direction. But there are many who criticize this idea, saying that creativity is of no use if it's not practical. Okay, granted, if it's part of our job, that's one thing. However, writing is a creative process. It need not always have a specific purpose, especially not when we're simply trying to get some words onto a blank page to explore an idea. Too often we put purpose before creativity and wind up going nowhere. While it's clear that our culture is all about practicality and efficiency, I'm certain that even in those artists' times there were similar expectations. If they had conformed, or inhibited themselves because they did not have someone's stamp of approval, then we would not be enjoying and praising their works today. We might not have even heard of them.

I love reading about artists who changed everything, the one's who took the risks to create what may have been incomprehensible to others of their time. When I go into an art museum today, I view art with a new set of eyes and try to understand what the artist was trying to convey and why. Art history provides me with a fresh resource that rouses the passion within me to be creative and write anyway!

Movies offer another way for me to find inspiration when

I'm unmotivated to write. I especially like to view the version with the director's and writer's commentary. When I discover how other creatives came up with their ideas, it fills me with inspiration. They took something that was nothing and turned it into art. How amazing is that? How inspiring is that?

I also love to read the biographies of authors to find out what or who inspired them, in order to discover what motivated them to keep writing. Knowing that others needed to find or even create their own inspiration is inspiring in and of itself.

So many readers have asked me how I keep writing every day, why I continue to write books and articles at such a rapid pace. It is because I am *compelled*. Something inside of me says I must write and so I do. Of course, it wasn't always that way. I guess what motivates me the most is that I want to make a difference. I want to help other people live better lives. And somehow, each and every day, I seem to come up with a new way to tell my story yet again, trying my best to encourage, motivate and inspire others. Whenever I learn something new, I try to share how it helped me.

The ultimate key for me though is that *I want to write*! Whether someone reads what I've written or not is secondary. When I finally stopped hiding behind my fears and admitted to myself that *I want to write—that yes, I am a writer*, that's when things changed. If it doesn't matter if anyone will read your work or not, that's acknowledgement that you want to do it for yourself first. If you decide later that you want to share your work, you may be pleasantly surprised when you find out what positive impact your writing may make.

I don't know what your specific inspiration and motivation is or will be, but perhaps reading about mine will give you some ideas. Throughout our lives, different things spark our interest, get us to look at the world in a different way, and ultimately inspire us to create or express ourselves through writing. It helps me to have a list of those things and keep it somewhere close for quick reference when I'm stuck.

Here's my list of inspiration generators that I use which help motivate me to write:

- Read a good book.
- Watch an interesting movie.
- Read an artist's bio.
- Read an author's bio.
- Read *anyone's* bio.
- Watch the producer, writer and director commentaries of my favorite movies to learn about their creative process.
- Ask fellow writers for their techniques and advice on how they get started, keep going and finish. (If nothing else, the conversation alone will whet your appetite to write.)
- Look at great art and imagine what the artist's inspiration was.
- Listen to particular music or songs that remind me of a great day or experience.
- Research revolutionaries from various fields, those individuals who broke the rules and created something new or unexpected.
- Read positive affirmations and reread thank you messages from my readers.
- Take photos and short notes of what I see and hear while out on long walks through the countryside.
- Seek out the positive in every situation. A setback may actually be a set up for something greater. In other words, when something doesn't work or go the way you want, examine how the results can be of benefit or what you can learn from the experience.

My most important motivation and inspiration comes from within. If we all look closely enough, I am sure that's where most of us will find it. Getting motivated sometimes takes an outside catalyst, as demonstrated by my list, but ultimately it's our inner desire that truly drives us. But motivation can look many different ways to many different people. While it's true I write for myself first, I must confess I also write because I want to make a difference and have a positive impact. If I'm honest, that is what now drives me each and every day. It means the entire world to me when someone writes me a short thank you note telling me that I somehow made a difference for them. I write to encourage people. I can't explain exactly why I want to encourage people so much. Perhaps it's because I wasn't encouraged enough when I was growing up. I had to find ways to believe in myself on my own while everything else seemed against me. Whenever I feel like I'm not a good enough writer, I take a moment to remember the brilliant teacher in that remedial reading and writing class. She was the one person who believed in me, the one person who was excited when I tried to spell my first word, and the one person who was thrilled when I wrote my first story.

However, when my professor told me I was never going to be a writer, I felt like I could give up forever. Maybe I would have if my therapist had not asked me to write my story, but I always knew someone believed in my writing. That's all I needed, and that's what I try to provide others. There are more than enough people who put us down and condemn even our best efforts; therefore, I can never write enough encouraging, positive material. Being able to help people keep going when they're completely discouraged makes it all worthwhile.

Find motivation and inspiration wherever you can. There's always something! *Purposely find it!* Don't wait for it to show itself because the odds are that it already has, and it may not have received the due attention and acknowledgement that it deserved. We can wait a lifetime for motivation and inspiration to find us, but it can take less than a day to transform our lives if we accept that it can come from within. It can come from a teacher or a kind word. Whatever it is, it's yours. The key is to purposely look for it and find it.

A few books I enjoy reading for inspiration are *You Are A Writer* by Jeff Goins, and *A Writer's Bucket List* by Dana Sitar. You can also download a book I wrote *Good Enough—Stop Seeking Perfection and Approval,* for free, just visit *PositiveWriter.com*

You Have the Potential

I believe you have the potential to be a writer because you're *passionate* about writing. It takes interest to light a spark, to start the journey, to learn, to be inclusive and to be a writer of any kind. But allow me to give you a little warning about potential—*potential is lost on those who are stuck in their own fears*, those who are afraid to be embarrassed or criticized. Don't let your potential go to waste without at least striving to reach it. Fear keeps us from reaching! Your greatness is within you, but first you have to overcome any internal fears and struggles you have about writing. Some of them, believe it or not, are instilled in us from perceptions that we have about what good writing is supposed to be.

Good writing, in my opinion, is about what I get from a story, what I learn from it, what new insights I gain about life. Good writing is interesting and compelling when someone decides to share his or her story with me.

If your story makes you feel *embarrassed*, you might be onto something. Don't let those feelings hold you back. While you were writing, did you learn something new about yourself? You could have found something readers will respond to. In the new readers' market people appreciate *reality writing* more than something contrived and formulaic.

What do I mean by reality writing? You've heard about reality TV, right? Well, the same thing goes for writing. Reality writing is telling your story the way it happened, the way you remember it—the good times, the bad times and the ugly times, in the way *you* write it, raw and real.

Again, I don't advise publishing something that is incomprehensible. For anyone planning to self-publish their work, I recommend finding a decent editor for a fair price. You don't need to spend thousands on editing, but you may need to spend a few hundred. I consider it essential to hire an editor with the right skills to correct typos, grammar, syntax, and to make sure what has been written is clear to the reader. I highly recommend this as the very basic editing to get for your book. Of course, it's *your* book so it's up to you. That's another great thing about self-publishing. You can do it your way.

Here is a list of the most common errors in self-published books that detract readers from fully enjoying a book:

- Spelling: Anyone who publishes a book in any manner really should ensure that their spelling is correct. Readers are not always forgiving of mistakes in spelling, especially if the errors are frequent. Many readers connect spelling with credibility. If an author does not ensure their spelling is correct, then how can the reader trust the information presented?

- Typos: Readers of self-published books are usually not that picky about one or two typos in an entire book, but if typos are found throughout the book then it can become frustrating to read. People who are frustrated while reading often stop and don't spread the word about the book.

- Repetition of words: My first drafts all too often repeat certain words over and over again. Sometimes certain words get stuck in our heads and whenever a certain type of sentence is being written that word will find a way to insert itself. Sometimes a certain word isn't necessary at all. Another, better word could be substituted. I don't consider repetition of words a mistake per se, but rather something that could detract from the overall content of the book. Speaking of which, how often can the word "certain" be used in a paragraph?

- Repetition of ideas: Just like with some words, ideas can get stuck in your heads, and you might repeat them several times without realizing it. Readers may then feel like you didn't think they could "get it" the first time. You or your editor can find such repetitions and either remove or combine them together. Keep in mind that even though you may repeat an idea, you might also include new information about the idea each time. You or your editor can add the new, useful information to a place in the book where you used the idea before and at the same time effectively remove the repetition.

- Organization: When writing a first draft it's mostly a matter of getting words onto the paper as they flow forth from us. Commonly the thoughts and ideas we write about don't come out of us in an organized manner, and as I mentioned above, we may repeat ourselves. An editor can help us organize our books to be more readable in a flowing, easy to follow manner.

- Punctuation: Even the best writers tend to make punctuation errors. A good editor will find them and correct them.

- Grammar: I am far from a grammar master. However, I can hire a grammar specialist to ensure my phrasing, word use and sentence structure is correct and readable.

The items above can all be corrected with basic editing at a relatively low cost. If you choose to skip this step, it's possible you will have a more difficult time getting your book to spread no matter how great the information. I think of editing as a tool to assist me in creating a book that is easy to read and effortless to understand. Most editors still might miss typos, grammar issues, and repetition. Take into consideration that it's common for traditional publishers to have more than one editor go over a manuscript. So if professionally trained editors can miss errors, how much, then, can self-published *authors* miss? It's better for trained editors to catch and correct what they can, rather than have someone's reading experience spoiled by basic errors that could have been corrected.

There's a difference between editing that ruins your voice and editing that corrects basic errors or typos for readability. The editing corrections I have presented will keep your particular writing style intact and won't rewrite your story. Some editors may like the information, but not the author's writing and therefore could decide to completely alter the work to the point that it becomes unrecognizable to the author. Some call such editing ghostwriting, rewriting or co-writing. Before hiring an editor it's important to be sure of what type of editing you want and to let the editor know exactly what to do. Being specific about what you want the editor to do could save you time, money and disappointment.

In order to make your style of writing as good and intelligible as possible, keep learning about writing. Never stop. I may have stopped going to formal classes, but I never stopped educating myself. Consider Steve Jobs, who dropped out of college but did not stop educating himself and would even attend classes after he dropped out.

Here's a short list of books I have read that have helped me continue to become a better writer:

- *English Grammar for Dummies* by Geraldine Woods
- *Idiot's Guide to Writing Well* by Laurie Rozakis, Ph.D.
- *Write On!* by Dan Mulvey, M.A.
- *100 Ways To Improve Your Writing* by Gary Provost
- *How To Write A Sentence* by Stanley Fish
- *On Writing—A Memoir of the Craft* by Stephen King
- *Bird by Bird* by Anne Lamott

I like to have a book about writing on my nightstand to read when I lie down, and I always have an audio book about writing queued up in my car. In these ways I learn about writing without any pressure. I'm learning while I am winding down for the night right before I go to sleep and during the quiet travel time in my car when I would normally be listening to songs I've heard over and over again.

Despite my unfortunate experiences with teachers, I still think it is very important to continue learning about writing in order to reach my full potential. Clearly, I'm not there yet. I don't know if I'll ever be, but I'll keep writing and keep learning.

We all learn differently, at our own pace, and not every teacher is optimally suited to teach you in the way you learn best. I was very lucky to experience at least one exceptional teacher for the way I learn. Had I never experienced her teaching method I may have come to believe I truly was hopeless. The right teacher for you can make all the difference. However, your continued education doesn't necessarily have to come from an academic "teacher." It could also come from a writing mentor or coach. I think we all know how we learn best. You've probably taken advantage of your specific learning style whether you recognized it or not. When you want to learn something enough, then you'll find the right way that suits you best. If you take advantage of continued learning either by reading about writing, or with the help of a mentor or a coach, your writing will benefit and so will your readers' experience.

Writing is Empowering

You have a story within you, but that story could be blocked by the story itself. There's a fear I mentioned briefly already, a fear that outranks all others. This fear is the reason too many repressed, would-be writers won't sit alone in a room and allow themselves the pleasure of forming words into sentences. It's the fear of telling one's true, personal story. Writing can bare our souls, our fears, and our anxieties. Our deepest terrors find voice in our writing. Internally, we all know that writing reveals everything about us, even our darkest secrets. But we aren't just afraid of revealing our story to the world. No, we can delete anything we write. We can burn our words, never to be read by anyone. Something else holds us back, blocking us from doing what we yearn to do.

Telling your story can be emotionally exhausting. Not the writing itself—the words may flow like a fountain, glorious and beautifully—but the memories we must visit, past sins we must admit, and the personal shame we must come to terms with that can hold us back. However, as hard as it is to write about the darkest parts of our story, writing can liberate us from the power they hold over us.

A writer once emailed me to explain he could not get his personal past out of his writing. In other words, every time he tried to write, memories of his past would be awakened and would be inadvertently inserted into his writing. This sounded so familiar to me that it was almost like déjà-vu. Before I wrote my memoir, I remember times when I tried to write short stories or articles and although I started with an entirely different subject, stories from my past would slip in. Others have emailed me over the years expressing nearly the same phenomenon, especially those who read my memoir and decided to write their own as a way to capture the thoughts which kept surfacing in a material form. The more I learn about the psychological aspects of writing, the less this surprises me. I'm not a psychologist, but I'll try to give you my take on this unique and puzzling mystery, or at least share my experience of the therapeutic benefits of writing my memoir and how it liberated me from haunting memories that demanded to be acknowledged. If you can't control your past from creeping into your writing, the solution is to write your past with *intention.*

When I wrote *One Boy's Struggle*, I had tears in my eyes during each writing session. I wrote about the things I could remember, but each word drew forth a new memory and another one after that. They came like a flood. Some nights I couldn't sleep. In fact, while writing my story there was an entire week that I didn't sleep for over 60 hours because I was facing too many repressed memories. I thought no one could ever understand. I couldn't even understand at first.

During that time I discovered something very important: writing can reveal the meaning behind our experiences. Yes, we remember things all the time, and we think we can see them clearly in our mind's eye, even to the point of actually feeling those things physically, such as with stomach aches or the constant, unexplained headaches I had for so long. Once we have things out of our heads and down on paper, it becomes possible to analyze them directly. Writing puts meaning to memories, meaning that may never be completely clear until we take the time and boldness to write about those memories.

For example, as I wrote my memoir I discovered I could stop blaming myself for all my failures as a child. For so many years I blamed myself for all of the things I did or did not do as a child. I thought I deserved to be severely punished. I was a bad kid, a terrible kid because I could not listen to instructions. I was often lost during classes because I was so distracted by my own thoughts. I believed my father's anger was exactly what I deserved.

However, when I wrote down my perceptions of what happened and how I felt during childhood, I was given the opportunity to see the truth of what I wrote. When I read back over my story, I had the opportunity to realize no child deserved to be treated the way I was. What I had always perceived to be the truth about myself wasn't the truth at all. I could finally stop blaming myself. Our writing can reveal what actually happened rather than what we perceived to have been the truth during the ordeals we lived through. And until we write intentionally about them, I think these repressed memories will insert themselves into our writing. Only when we deal with them can we move forward.

Didn't I deserve to be repeatedly punished as a child? Didn't I deserve the wrath that was brought down upon me? Shouldn't a small child know what life is all about and the importance of acting "normal?" If a young child doesn't understand the significance of performing well at school and home, then obviously he is an unmitigated disaster in the making, and he should be punished severely. And if he cries the tears of a small boy, then he is a poor, pathetic child indeed. Don't you think? Doesn't it all make sense?

One Boy's Struggle is what finally set me free mentally and emotionally from the burden of blame I had placed upon myself. Because of my internal confusion at such a young age, this blame had played on in my head for most of my life. Some may wonder to themselves how it's possible for an adult to fail to comprehend the truth, but every writer who has written about his or her personal history knows that regardless of what we *should* understand, it doesn't mean that the small child within us does. At last, after writing my memoir, the truth was revealed in my story, not only to readers around the world who would eventually read it but, more importantly, to me.

It doesn't matter how smart or experienced we become, that little child inside each of us has a story to tell. Unfortunately, many of us block ourselves from facing what our inner child may reveal and avoid writing our story. It is so important to intentionally write our story because our inner child will continue to try to speak until it's heard. This, then, is why our past sneaks into our writing. This is what inhibits us from writing more regularly, the fear of exposing ourselves to unpleasant memories.

Many of us know there is that moment in our past that we're ashamed of or deeply regret. We wish we could put that moment behind us forever and completely forget about it, but the truth I realized is that we never will until we discover the truth about our pasts. Writing helps us do that.

Writing is powerful, but it can also be terrifying. Writing makes us think, writing makes us consider, and writing makes us explore within. We cannot always control where our thoughts may venture, what doors they may knock on and what we may find on the other side of those doors. However, it's very difficult to freely write anything until we have written our story for ourselves. Whether we realize it or not, our personal story may always attempt to insert itself into the things we write. And when this happens, we may stop and become blocked, fearful of going back to writing, even if we don't realize why.

Write to understand and to move forward. Write for empowerment. Don't let the fears of years gone by hold you back from doing what you truly want to do. I never understood what was really blocking me from writing. I thought it was because others had put me down and told me that I would never be a writer, but that wasn't the complete truth. Instead, I used what they said to hold *myself* back because I knew whenever I started putting words to paper I was visiting places I wasn't ready to visit. I did not understand the clarity I would gain from writing about the things that had happened in my life. I didn't understand that the child who I had been so many years before was still inside of me and needed to tell his story. After writing *One Boy's Struggle,* I understand my story because I understand his story.

If you want to write, I truly believe you should write. And yes, all the anxieties, memories, and dread you felt then may come to the surface and present themselves undiluted, but this can be a good thing, providing you the opportunity to re-evaluate the darkest memories you have with all you have learned over the years. If you're as fortunate as I was, you will free yourself of old fears that no longer serve any purpose, empowering your writing and liberating your life at once.

You have probably heard the saying that artists are always suffering to express their art. I think that's because they are trying to tell their story, but words do something no other art form can: they directly communicate memories and experiences that can be read and more clearly understood. Keep in mind, the only reason anyone (including me) will ever understand my memories, beliefs and experiences is because *I actually wrote about them.* This gave me the opportunity to reexamine my past and finally, truly understand what actually happened.

I did touch on this topic earlier, but I would like to say again that if you have suffered trauma, these memories may be overwhelming. If you decide to write your story, consider using the support of a therapist. While I wrote *One Boy's Struggle*, my therapist was able to clarify my most painful memories and help me see the reality within my story. I was not at fault for what another person did and that even under such crushing and confusing circumstances I was a survivor who found his own ways to cope and overcome. By examining my written past, I learned a lot about myself, my abilities and my worth.

Writing Rituals

If you're still struggling to write and you already know what you want to write about, but doubt still asserts its control over you, then it will help if you develop writing rituals.

I know the term "writing rituals" runs counter to the idea that we shouldn't follow strict, traditional rules, but actually that's not the case at all. Writing rituals are widely used by almost every type of writer. And many prolific writers who get into their writing zone rather easily typically use them even if they never take a moment to notice them. Let's be honest, all writers want to write frequently, every day if they can, but if we look too closely at the reasons we don't write every day, we might jinx ourselves, lose our focus, or even lose our inspiration.

However, writing rituals make writing easy, a habit that comes on its own. The two hardest parts of writing is arguably starting and finishing. When I actually started finishing writing projects, I noticed that I had made writing a part of my daily routine. This routine or ritual has been the ultimate key for me to finish what I start writing. I am not talking about a step-by-step program. Since every writing project is different, I don't buy into any step-by-step writing program. They've never worked for me anyway. However, if I follow my daily writing rituals, I know I am going to write tomorrow, and this knowledge ultimately helps me get into the right frame of mind more quickly so I can focus on what I want to write about.

If we really think about it, too much of our time is often spent figuring out how we're going to find time to write or hoping that the urge to write will soon come over us. Rituals take away the guesswork and allow for the actual process of creation to develop instead of wasting valuable time.

Professionals in nearly every profession and sport use rituals, and most of us have rituals we follow from the very moment we wake up in the morning to the time we go to bed. Our rituals help us stay on track to do the things we need to do every day. If you can incorporate your writing into your daily rituals you will find it much easier to write every day.

I have particular rituals I use to keep myself writing on a daily basis. In the morning, I get up, brush my teeth and take a shower. Then I head to the kitchen where I know I can find hot coffee. My wife is so awesome she makes the coffee every morning! I pour myself a cup and then go directly to my writing desk. Since I have started writing on a daily basis, I make it a point to wake up at least two hours before I go to work or do errands. These two hours become my writing time, and I guard it carefully. If I only have an hour, I feel too crunched for time and cannot find the inspiration I need. I spend half-an-hour reading emails and replying to the most pressing ones. Then, I stand up and walk around the living room for a moment or two just to think. Walking helps me generate and process ideas. If I keep staring at the computer screen I won't be able to begin, or I'll get distracted visiting websites. Still, as I walk, I have to be very careful because I might end up getting distracted with a task around the house and miss writing for the entire day. After my brain is warmed up from my little walk around the living room I come back to my desk. With my ritual complete, I can immediately start writing.

I have repeated my morning ritual so many times I now do it on autopilot. It's quite simple, but it has proven extremely effective. I worry less about not writing and do a heck of a lot more of it, and this freedom from creative anxiety is why I think it's important to have a set time each day for writing and make it part of your ritual. You and your writing will benefit, and so will your readers because they will have more to read from you.

Here are a few ways to create consistent writing rituals:

- Set a time and place for writing every day.
- Do the same actions in the same order every day when preparing to write.
- If you enjoy tea, coffee, or any favorite beverage or snack while you write, then make sure preparing it is part of your

ritual, too.
- Each day, write for the same amount of time. A little variance is fine but not too much. That being said, if you have the chance to write all day, take it!
- Create a routine that is natural and comfortable for you. Each person's personal rhythms and schedules are different. Morning might not be the right time for you. The best time is probably when you can focus best and won't be interrupted.
- Keep your rituals as simple as possible.

    What you want is for your writing to become a habit and to become a part of your life. When you commute to work, you do it naturally. You don't have to think about where you're going or how long it will take to get there. You just do it. The first time you took your commute, you may have worried about traffic, signs, and lights, but after time it became as routine as breathing. Rituals create the same mindset for writing, and that's exactly what you want. When you stop focusing on the writing process itself, writing becomes as second nature as driving your car. When it's second nature, you're much less likely to stall.

    My daily writing ritual did not develop over night. It was created over time, through trial and error. I didn't even know that I was creating a routine. However, as soon as I did realize I was naturally creating a ritual, I started to purposely do things in a more thought-out, consistent way. I think it's important as writers for us to take notice of what we're doing naturally, adding to our routine slowly but purposely. If you don't have a writing ritual yet, then perhaps what I have shared here will save you some time creating yours.

    I still get anxious when I start writing a new book or blog post; I've learned this is normal. We each must find ways to overcome such feelings because if we don't have writing rituals, those feelings can easily lead to writing paralysis. However, I still do get stuck sometimes, and so I've created the following list of things help get me unstuck.

- Take an extended break for a couple days and not write at all.
- Take a very long walk and try not to think about what I am writing. I have discovered that when I do this thoughts and ideas will start coming to me without my beckoning them.
- Do something that relaxes me and gets my mind off of my writing worries. One of those things is to go out with my wife and visit a zoo, an unfamiliar city, or a new art museum. My wife is a very fun person to be around so she easily helps me get my mind off of writing.
- Drink a large glass of cool water. We may not realize it, but we can easily forget to hydrate when we write. Drinking pure water helps with focus and clear thinking, and it also helps relieve feelings of anxiousness.

Sometimes I simply need to get away from writing for a period of time. I've discovered this is okay. There were times when I would waste hour after hour staring at the screen hoping inspiration would come to me. That never worked, though, and I'd get further upset because I had wasted so much time doing nothing. So you might find it's better to get up and get away for a while.

Many people find writing retreats inspiring, but when I go somewhere I have not been before I get easily distracted by the newness of the place and just end up feeling unsettled. Instead, I write at home every day because it's where I feel most comfortable. My desk is my oasis. However, people are different, some have too many distractions at home and need to get away to write. That's fine, but if you can't get away regularly then you might not write that often. My advice here is to create a little writing sanctuary in your home. Perhaps it's in your bed, or maybe it's in your attic or basement. Find a place that is the least distracting for you, a place you can always go to write.

To further kick-start your writing, sometimes it's a good idea to have writing prompts nearby. A good book that can help is *The Write Practice: 14 Prompts* by Joe Bunting.

The Zone

Rituals help me get in the writer's zone, but I have also discovered other ways that help me get into the zone and overcome Writer's Doubt.

When I'm in the writer's zone, words come effortlessly. No need for pauses or extended breaks to mull over an idea. No need to worry about whether something is written to perfection or not. I can write what I want to write to my heart's content, without any constraints whatsoever. It's heaven. When I come out of the writer's zone, it's amazing to look back over so many pages and see so much text. I often find myself bewildered about how much I wrote. Where in the world did those ideas come from? What's more is that my errors seem to be fewer than normal, ideas and thoughts are well presented and over all, it's an awe-inspiring experience. I write every day, but I write my best when I am in the zone.

Here are a few techniques I use to get in to 'the zone':

- Background noise helps me a great deal to get into my writing zone. However, when I use the word "noise," I don't mean just any noise. I mean sounds that I enjoy, but are not distracting. They are there, soothing my brainwaves so to speak, but I hardly notice them. Instrumental music works effectively, but it must be very familiar and not have any notes that are so striking that they will take me out of focus. You've probably already heard of this and may have heard the terms, background noise or white noise, but if the sound is soothing to you, is it really noise? For example, noise that comes from outside that is obnoxious or discordant and is pretty much just banging around, that's rather annoying and distracting to me. The sounds that I listen to in the background must be mild and pleasant.

- Meditation before writing helps send me into the writer's zone, too. If you haven't tried meditation then you may be surprised at how well silencing the mind can generate thoughts and ideas about what you want to write. A few times a week, I try to take a half hour of free time to meditate. I need to be alone in a place where I am comfortable and know I won't be disturbed. Meditation isn't always easy, especially if you don't already meditate regularly. I highly recommend finding a good instructor who can help you learn how to meditate correctly if you don't already have experience. You can also purchase very good audiotapes that will guide you through the meditation process. If you're familiar with meditation and are comfortable with it, then you may want to do what I do before I start: I close my eyes and ask myself questions about what I am going to write. This helps my mind generate ideas while I am meditating. I consider the writer's zone an actual form of meditating *while* writing when words can simply flow without any sort of hindrance.

- From time to time I add Tai Chi to my morning rituals. Tai Chi exercises are deliberate movements and controlled breathing. By doing Tai Chi for a few minutes I can condition my body to breathe correctly before I start writing. I am an amateur at Tai Chi, but it still helps me considerably. I sometimes wonder how much it would help if I ever take the time to become good at it.

- Taking a walk through nature helps me come up with new ideas on how to proceed with my current writing, or a new writing project. Similar to meditating, I like to use the first half of my walk talking to myself, asking questions. During the second half of my walk, I'll stop talking and try to completely clear my mind. This helps my mind relax and take in the questions I asked and hopefully give me the answers I will need to write. A word of caution about this, though. Sometimes on my walk back home, I suddenly have a great idea but have nowhere to write it down. I have been so far away without anything to write that I forgot what my great idea was by the time I got home. So the lesson for me is to always, always have my notebook with me—or at least my cell phone—just in case I have an epiphany.

- Sometimes before I fall asleep at night I'll picture myself sitting at my computer, attentively typing. I'll see pages of my writing flowing like a river, with a constant current that never slows or pauses. I imagine it in continuous, steady motion, and the writing keeps coming. I see myself doing what I love to do, thoroughly enjoying it and fall asleep with those visions still playing in my mind. These visualizations often help me get into the writer's zone, and when I remember to create these visualizations before I fall asleep, the next day I may have a fantastic day in the zone.

Creating your "zone" does take some effort. You will want to experiment with these or similar methods to discover what works best for you. Sometimes these techniques work and sometimes they don't, but I have noticed that the more often I use them, the more I find myself in the zone.

Slaying *The Beast*

Writer's Doubt is insidious. What makes it so challenging to overcome is that it comes from within us. Yes, there are people who have criticized our writing and told us in one way or another that we're not good enough. Some of us have even had teachers or editors tell us to give it up. But their words are nothing compared to the harshest critic of all, ourselves.

Nobody can be as hard on you as you can. You know your fears and frustrations better than anyone. Haters can try all day to put you down, but their efforts, although still hurtful, don't stop you from writing for long. Every once in a while, a critic may say something that hits the mark, the proverbial bull's-eye, causing you to stop writing and consider giving up. However, *you know your triggers* and anytime your internal naysayer's voice rises up to make you doubt yourself, she hits her mark every, single, time.

You are a writer. You know it, and I know it. You have the power to overcome doubt, and you can do it. Believe it. You have stories within you that you absolutely need to share with the world and there are people who need to read them. So, don't hide. No. Please don't hide your writing. It's true, not everyone will "get you," but that's okay. Not everyone "gets" Stephen King, either, and he's still sold over 350 million copies of his books. Once you accept that, Writer's Doubt will loosen its grip. We give critics, haters, and those who don't like our writing way too much power. Here's the truth: THEY DESERVE ABSOLUTELY NO POWER OVER YOU.

Take away your internal naysayer's power over you. The next time it starts whispering its sweet *you-can-do-nothings*, stop what you're doing and state with conviction "I am a writer". And it will whimper off and wait to try again another day. And yes, it will try again. It knows your secrets, even the dirty ones, and it will use them against you. But each time it tries, it will fail if you state, "I am a writer," and continue to write. Your internal naysayer is a dark, shadowy lurker, and the way to force darkness away is to shine a light on it. It's that simple. And it's that difficult. For example, maybe you're not too happy with a piece of writing you did in the past (you know the piece I am talking about). You recently read it, realized how terrible it was, and then told yourself you're really not that good of a writer. Stop. Repeat after me, "I am a writer!" It was your naysayer playing tricks on you. Of course, as I stated earlier, we all look upon our past writing with fresh eyes and realize it's not as good as what we could write today. That's normal, and it's a positive affirmation, because as time progresses we learn to improve as writers. But if your doubt convinces you that you're a terrible writer, you risk giving in and quitting writing altogether.

See how sinister Writer's Doubt can be? I've fallen for such trickery from it, and maybe you have, too. The good news is that once you realize what's happening you don't have to fall for it anymore. You are a writer. Go ahead, say it again, right now, "I am a writer."

To help you reach your goal of overcoming Writer's Doubt I've put together a summary of strategies from what I've already mentioned and additional strategies I believe will help you.

- Accept that writing is about writing, nothing more and nothing less, it's not about being perfect. You don't have to be the next Hemingway. You get to be someone unique and rare. You get to be you. So, be the matchless, remarkable you.

- Write the story you fear to write, the story within you, the story *about you*. You don't need to share this story with anyone if you don't want to, but write it anyway. Write about your fears, your guilt and everything you might feel ashamed about. Our doubts have the most power when they remain hidden from ourselves, but when we write about them we can expose them for what they really are, voices we no longer need to hide from or submit to. As writers, when we write about our fears we give ourselves the rare ability to print them, read and understand them and then, put them in a box and say these words, "I understand and appreciate these concerns, but they have no power over me anymore." and finally, place a lid on the box to symbolize regaining your power over your fears. One day you may want to share your story about your fears with the world as I am doing in this book, but the important thing is that you've written their story, effectively taking control of their power over you.

- Take control of the critic within you by recognizing if and when you criticize other writers. When we're overly critical of other writers, we're often projecting our own doubts. After all, if you doubt your own writing, it can cause you to be overly critical, and even cruel. It's not you. It's your own doubt saying, "Don't be fooled by this person's inferior writing, as if that gives you permission to write. His writing is drivel." The next thing you know you're writing a harsh review or commenting negatively on their blog post. Confident writers still recognize writing that needs work, but they use grace and kindness to coach fellow writers to help them become better. Isn't that what you would want from fellow writers? So, consider being kind and helpful to other writers. No matter what level their writing might be, remember they are doing all they can to overcome their own Writer's Doubt, too. In helping them overcome Writer's Doubt, you'll help yourself at the same time. Keep in mind that it's only a good idea to give feedback when it's asked for and not unsolicited. Unsolicited feedback, no matter how well intended, is almost always regarded as negative. If you have noticed a typo, misspelling or something else, ask the author if they want your input first, and let the writer know that your only intention is to be helpful. If they say yes, then go for it, and if they say no, then move on and don't force your input.

- Write down positive affirmations, and put them everywhere so you'll see them constantly. When I turn on my computer monitor there's a bold statement next to the "On" button that states, "I am a writer." It's true, *I am a writer*, and turning on my monitor is like turning on myself to begin writing. Consider positive affirmations as spotlights that you shine upon your internal naysayer.

- Limit the people who you share your writing with to only those you trust to give you honest and helpful feedback. When you publish your work on your blog or in magazines, newspapers, or books, the whole world can read and comment on your writing. But while you're still in the process of writing, you want to guard your work from overzealous critics, and especially from others so riddled with their own doubt that they feel the need to tear yours apart. This doesn't mean you want dishonest feedback, but you do want feedback you can work with and use to improve your writing. Share your writing with people you deem helpful, people you see as coaches and mentors. Coaches and mentors help you hone and improve your writing by identifying places that need work, but they also let you know what is working. In the end, they encourage you to continue writing rather than feeding your inner doubt.

- Don't compare yourself to other writers. All of us are at different levels, some are better and some are worse. Some attract tons of attention while others, even better writers, attract very little. Comparing yourself to other writers serves no one because there's nothing to gain from it. It's too easy to compare yourself to others, to start thinking negative thoughts about how it's not fair that a less talented writer made the bestseller list or that you'll never be as good a writer as someone else. It just doesn't matter, and your own doubt will always distort the comparison in order to stall your writing. Remember, you're the only one with your voice and style, and you're the only one who can write your story the way you tell it. No one can be you. People have spent years trying to write like others, to copy their style and their voice, but ultimately everyone is unique. So don't ever be afraid to be you or think that your story has been told a thousand times before, because although there may be other stories like it, none of them are yours.

- Write something dangerous. Write what you want to write, and don't hold back. Be honest, and remember, honesty is always dangerous. Challenge the status quo, challenge yourself and challenge the critics who said you can't write.

Take a stand and write something meaningful, honest, and, as a result, something that matters. This is the best type of writing to help you overcome Writer's Doubt. Strive to write something dangerous every day.

- Find out what inspires you, whether they are places, items, certain art, or even people. It could be watching movies, listening to music, dancing, or simply going for a swim in a nearby lake. The same way that we have triggers for negative feedback from our critic within, we also have triggers for inspiration and motivation. Identify all the things that inspire you and make a list of them, use an item from your list daily to keep you going, to keep you writing work that matters. If taking a walk inspires you to write, then plan to take walks regularly. If visiting museums helps, then locate museums near you and visit whenever you can. When you're overcome with doubt it can be hard to remember what inspires you, so make your list and add to it whenever you discover a new inspiration.

- Don't wait to be picked. If you have been waiting for an agent or traditional publisher to pick you and the wait has caused you to doubt yourself even more, then it's time to stop waiting to be picked. Self-publishing is easier than it has ever been, and rather than being a limitation on your success, it can actually be a way to get your writing in front of more eyes than ever before. I'll provide some tips on self-publishing in the next chapters, but know this, you don't have to wait to be picked.

- Write intentionally. Writer's Doubt causes us to stall, to hold back our stories, and to find distractions that keep us from writing. The only way to overcome distractions is to be intentional, to write every day, rain or shine. You might write 500 words one day and 2000 the next. The length doesn't matter. Just be intentional, and write every day.

- Establish writing rituals. To write intentionally on a daily basis it helps to have established writing rituals. Rituals save time and give the voice inside of your head less opportunity to interrupt you and cause you to stall. If you follow your writing rituals for an extended time, they will become habits you don't need to think about anymore. You just do them.

- Break out of your comfort zone and write about something different, totally unrelated to anything you've written before. For years, I maintained one blog in a very specific niche and didn't write about anything else because I didn't think I was good enough. But over the years I've learned a lot about writing, creativity, blogging and publishing. I wanted to share what I learned with others, but Writer's Doubt consistently talked me out of starting a new blog by stating silly things like, "You have no education. You're a drop out, a failure and your writing sucks." Yep, my inner critic grew so confident that it became as snarky as it was sinister. For a long time, I allowed it to win because I postponed starting my new blog. Finally, I overcame my doubt and started, Positive Writer. I did what I wanted, but feared to do. And to my astonishment only a few months after starting *Positive Writer*, the blog started winning awards. Soon I was guest posting on the most popular writing blogs, such as *The Write Practice, Write to Done, Goins Writer,* and *Helping Writers Become Authors*, among others. Doubt can talk us out of doing what we really want to do, if you let it, but when you strive to overcome it and step out of your comfort zone amazing things can happen.

- Write a letter to yourself. So far we've talked mostly about Writer's Doubt, but there's another side of yourself, too, and that other side gives you positive reinforcement. Whenever you overcome doubt it's because the positive side gained the upper hand and gave you the courage to write. There should be balance between the negative and positive sides of yourself, but for most people, the negative "you-can't-do-it" side wins 90% of the time because it's an attention getter. It knows how to use your deepest fears against you. However, you can help your positive side develop a stronger voice that can balance out the negative. A great way to do this is to write a letter to yourself from the positive side within you.

Listen to those nurturing words in your head and write them on a piece of paper in the form of a letter to yourself. You may be surprised to find that you already have all the answers you need to overcome doubt. Keep the letter in a safe place and read it whenever you begin to feel doubt taking over again.

- Learn from your failures and mistakes because that's what they're there for. Everyone fails and everyone makes mistakes. Too many of us have an unrealistic belief that we should not make any mistakes and that if we fail then we aren't good enough. It's not true. You can't grow as a writer, or in any endeavor for that matter, if you don't make mistakes. None of us were born knowing everything. When you were a baby, and you failed to walk the first time, your parents didn't give up on you. No, they allowed you to try again and again until you could walk. So why is it you're so hard on yourself? Doubt. That's why. Doubt magnifies and exaggerates everything negatively. As a baby learning how to walk, you didn't know what doubt was yet, so you tried again no matter how many times you fell. Doubt turns our mistakes and failures into end-all-be-alls, but instead, they're just ways that didn't work. Thomas Edison didn't give up when he created 10,000 light bulbs that failed to work. So why is it so easy for our mistakes to stop us from writing?

- Refuse to blend in and conform. Too many writers allow doubt to control them by writing work that blends in. You will never set yourself apart if you're writing what everyone else is writing the way everyone else is writing it. Put your personal spin on whatever you write, even if you're writing about a subject that's already widely explored.

- Give your first draft the credit it deserves. You can't write a final draft if you never write a first draft. It's the most essential draft you will ever write. Don't look down on your first draft. Just write it.

- Highlight your successes. With all this talk about Writer's

Doubt, it's important to remember it doesn't always win. You have achievements too. It's time to give them credit and remind yourself of them when you're feeling discouraged. On my wall above my desk I have a two-page spread article from a magazine that was reviewing one of my books. I keep it there to remind myself that my writing matters. Whenever I start doubting whether my work will be published, I simply look up and remind myself that I already am published! If I've already done it, then there's no reason I can't do it again. If you've already written a story, there's no reason you can't write another. Your successes remind you that "you can do it," even when your naysayer is trying to convince you that you can't.

- Reward yourself when you start *and* when you finish a project. One of the goals of Writer's Doubt is to steal any joy you have from writing. It wants you to feel like writing is about as much fun as getting your teeth pulled. The way to defeat this attack on your joy and confidence is to reward yourself whenever you start a project. Treat yourself to dinner in a nice restaurant or go someplace special that you only visit when you're feeling your best. When you finish your project, reward yourself again, perhaps by something even grander (like treating yourself to dinner *and* a movie). Writer's Doubt can't make you stop writing if you're celebrating the fact that you *are* writing.

- Don't underestimate yourself. You are better than you think you are. Yes. You are. Doubt has this unique way of convincing you that you're not capable of anything. It can affect you to the point that you not only underestimate your abilities, you discredit them. It starts out as a small voice in your head saying things like, "I'll never be that good," "I don't have what it takes," "I don't have the training, the education, the luck or the skill." It can become so self-deprecating you no longer trust your ability to hold a pen. If you don't completely give up, you stop giving your best, stop taking the necessary risks to improve. If you've ever heard those statements in your head, be particularly wary, because they are not true. It's your internal naysayer guised under the cover of saving you from letdown. It's deceivingly stealing your confidence. This particular deception of Writer's Doubt is especially devious, because it gives you what seem like legitimate excuses for not writing and living up to our potential. "The odds are against you, you're not the lucky type and besides, you're tired of fooling yourself and wasting time." Right? If this sounds familiar to you, know that your naysayer is the cause and it's time to defeat it and the way to defeat it is to write anyway despite its yammering. Doubt itself does not underestimate you, because it knows you're capable of greatness. No. Doubt's goal is to convince you that you're not capable of greatness by causing you to not only underestimate yourself, but to get you to discredit any chances you might have even if you tried.

- Practice writing in public. Now, when I say write in public I don't mean go to Starbucks and write—which is fine, by the way. What I really mean is share your writing publicly. And do it frequently. A blog is a great way to do this. (I'll share a few tips with you about blogging soon.) If you have a blog or even an online writer's community where you can post your writing, it's a great way to get yourself to write frequently, and as I am sure you know, the only way to get better at writing is to write as often as possible. The one thing that doubt detests more than you actually writing is having the spotlight shined on it. So it stands to reason that one of the best ways to overcome Writer's Doubt is to share your writing publicly.

- The most important tip of all: If you're to the point that Writer's Doubt is sabotaging your every effort, then that means you're on to something awesome! Writer's Doubt is at its loudest when you're about to make a major breakthrough. Keep moving forward, keep writing, doubt can't stop you anymore. You'll know this because it will go nuts trying every weapon in its arsenal to make you stop. You know how just after it rains, when the clouds clear and the sky seems to brighten up with sunshine brighter than ever before. That's what it's like after you finish your masterpiece in spite of doubt's efforts to trip you up. It's worth it. Trust me, it really is. You're going to make it after all. You are a writer!

If one of the strategies above doesn't work for you today, try a different one, and keep trying them until you find the balance that works for you. These strategies are easy to use, but if Writer's Doubt has a firm grip on you then they may seem much more difficult than they should be. If you do a few of them consistently, I know you'll overcome Writer's Doubt.

Dealing with and overcoming rejection.

The mere thought of rejection has caused more writers nightmares than probably any other fear. Unfortunately, as a writer you'll have to deal with rejection eventually. Let's be honest, if you seek to be published in newspapers, magazines and in books via traditional publishers, the odds are you will get rejected. That's okay. It's happened to the best. It happened to Stephen King, J. K. Rowling and even Dr. Seuss. It's probably going to happen to you. I am not going to tell you to simply get over it. Instead, I have a few tips on how to deal with it.

1. Admit it, getting rejected sucks. Go ahead, just tell yourself right now, "Getting rejected sucks and hurts like hell." Because it does, on both counts. No writer worth his or her salt is completely immune to the pain rejection delivers.

2. Grieve. The next step is to allow your emotions room to breathe. You need to give yourself permission to grieve intentionally. There's nothing worse than needing to express your pain and holding it in. Go somewhere, perhaps in the middle of the woods, and just scream. It's okay. You don't want to bottle up your emotions inside because if you don't let them out doubt will use them against you. If screaming isn't your thing and you feel like crying, then by all means get a pillow, some chocolate or ice cream and cry your heart out. You'll feel better. Trust me, I'm writing from experience.

3. Persevere. Doubt loves rejection. It thrills in the chance to tell you "I told you so." This is why letting your emotions out is

imperative, and the sooner, the better. I don't suggest forcing your emotions because they have their own timetable, but when you do feel them allow them to run their course. Now, here's what to watch for: While your emotions are at their height, doubt will start whispering in your ear. Her voice may be soothing. She may tell you everything will be okay, that you knew it was going to happen anyway. Doubt will continue her sweet whispers saying things like, "You don't need to deal with this anymore," "you should never try again because the pain just isn't worth it," "besides, no one cares enough to understand what you're writing about," "they don't deserve your words." As comforting as that may sound, doubt has only one goal, and that is to get you to give up, to quit trying to be published and to stop you from striving to improve as a writer.

4. Keep writing. As you grieve, you'll come to a point where it's time to stop grieving. No matter what, keep writing, keep improving and continue to send your work out. If you were fortunate to get feedback with your rejection notice, read it closely and see if you can learn something valuable from it. If you sent your manuscript to only one agent or publisher, or even a few, it's time to send it to a dozen more. Dr. Seuss' first book was rejected well over twenty times!

5. Write for love. You love writing. You do it first and foremost for you. Getting published was, is, and always will be, a byproduct of doing what you love. It's great when it happens, but it's not why you started writing. You will get better and you will continue to send your work out no matter what, but if you always do it because you love to write, doubt won't be able to talk you out of it. Write for you. Write because you love to write. Love always trumps doubt.

6. Self-publish. If rejection ever gets so overwhelming that you sincerely consider giving up, don't. Instead consider self-publishing your work. If there's a market for your writing you will find it. And if you do choose to self-publish that may be your road to get traditionally published. I self-published *One Boy's Struggle* and since then two traditional

publishers have approached me about publishing it. While I turned them down, maybe one will come along with an offer I can't refuse. I don't know, but I don't regret self-publishing it for a second. It turned out that self-publishing was the right path for me. Doubt will always try to convince you that rejection is bad and nothing good can come from it, but that's not true. I learned that things happen for reasons and in one way or another, those reasons benefit us in some way. In what ways will rejection benefit you? I don't know, but I do know you have to intentionally look for them.

Part II – BONUS CHAPTERS on Self-publishing, Blogging and Marketing

So far I have discussed how I overcome Writer's Doubt and write every day. I hope what I have written will help you overcome your doubts, too. But I want to share more of my writing journey with you with regard to self-publishing, blogging and marketing. Consider the following chapters as bonus chapters with basic tips from my personal experiences.

You might be wondering what these topics have to do with overcoming doubt. One of the best ways of overcoming doubt that I know of is to always keep moving forward, always keep going to the next level and never stay stagnate for too long. The next step forward could be to create a blog where you practice your writing in public or publishing your book. Few things have helped me overcome doubt more than practicing in public.

Publish Anyway

Getting your work published can be a very emotional and taxing experience, but it doesn't have to be that way.

If you want your work to be traditionally published it will require a lot of time, dedication and persistence. The odds are that you will receive a great number of rejection notices. I say that without knowing you and without having any idea whether you've written the best book in the world or not, and *that's the point*. Many publishers may say "No, thank you." without ever actually reading your work. You may also be rejected because they aren't sure how well your writing will fit into the current market. Try to keep in mind that it's never personal and is often a matter of perceived market value. That's where self-publishing becomes a more viable alternative. You can prove your book's market value through self-publishing, and if you do prove it, you may attract a traditional publisher. You may even find that you have more success on your own than you would have had if you'd gone with the first publisher who said "Yes."

When I submitted *One Boy's Struggle* to publishers, one editor told me it would never be published the way it was written, that no one would buy it, much less read it. I can't tell you how devastating that was to hear. My memoir was the first real writing I had completed since that professor had told me I would never be a writer. So I now had two experts in the field make it abundantly clear to me that I couldn't do it! You might think that would have been enough to get me to give up. Who would blame me? In decades past, such a message could have been a death knell to someone like me. However, I can't say enough about how blogging and self-publishing has provided opportunities for many who otherwise would never have their work published, or much less, find readers. It's becoming more obvious that "experts" don't always speak for the public at large.

I'll admit that I did decide to allow my memoir to be edited to "perfection" because of the rejections. And when I finally received the improved, edited version, I did not recognize the book as mine anymore. It was so perfectly edited, that I couldn't recognize my style or my voice. My memoir read like a novel and I couldn't feel a connection with my own story. It was my story, but it wasn't *me*. The editing cost a fortune, but I threw it in the trash and decided to self-publish the original version, only fixing typos and glaring mistakes. Eventually my memoir became the bestselling book of the self-publisher I used, Infinity publishing. It was a gamble, to be sure, but I sincerely believe that when readers want to read real life stories, they prefer them in the author's own words, raw and real. But that's me, and, of course, I could have been wrong. Thankfully self-publishing gave me the opportunity to find out.

I don't know if the edited version, which amounted to a full rewrite, would have done well in the new readers' market or not, and I don't know if a traditional publisher or an agent would have been more likely to accept it that way. However, I do know that my book in its original form is becoming considered a "must read" and many authorities in my niche have praised it in reviews and hailed it as the "story that needed to be told." Pulitzer Prize winning journalist, Katherine Ellison, author of *Buzz*, says my book is a "very brave and moving memoir". CHADD educator of the year (2010), Dr. Katherine Nell McNeil, highly recommends it to teachers and parents. Not only do many well-known names in my niche highly value it, but so too have a large number of readers. On Amazon *One Boy's Struggle* has received dozens of five-star reviews, as well as five-star reviews on my publisher's online bookstore. I have received hundreds of "thank you" emails from readers all over the world, and my book is only available *in English!* In June 2011 my publisher, Infinity Publishing, sent out a newsletter listing me as one of their three bestselling authors.

I sincerely believe the edited version wouldn't have had the impact that *One Boy's Struggle* is having in its original form. To the editor who said no one would publish it, I say, "*I* can, and I did." Gone are the publishing house gatekeepers.

For so long self-publishing was considered by many as second-rate, only an alternative for those who were "not good enough" to get their work traditionally published. However, the market is clearly changing, and as books become more popular in downloadable formats most readers won't try to discern which one is self-published or traditionally published. A book they want to read will simply be that, and there won't be as much scrutiny or concern about how it was published or by what company. Remember the shock Rebecca Black gave to the music industry that I mentioned earlier? Her self-published music video "Friday" became the most popular song in the world practically overnight! Self-publishing is clearly not what it used to be before the Internet made it possible to reach the masses without vast amounts of money or media coverage.

I will admit that I think authors should first try to get their work traditionally published. Traditional publishers can distribute a book more effectively to brick-and-mortar stores, cover the entire costs of publishing, and provide valuable services to authors including editing, marketing, printing in foreign languages and much more. I have had hundreds of requests for my memoir in various languages, and I simply don't have the resources to oblige them. Furthermore, people do still like to browse their local bookstore. That part of the industry, I believe, will always be important. I would like to have *One Boy's Struggle* in bookstores all over the world, but as a self-published book it's nearly impossible for me to get it in bookstores unless I actually go store-to-store asking them to carry it. That said, many traditionally published books never make it into bookstores, either. Self-publishing has come very far and over the next decade, and I expect it's going to become an even more popular option for authors. Traditional publishers still have the distinct edge, but the edge is getting hazier by the year.

Another important factor to consider about traditional publishers is they have valuable experience. They've owned the publishing business for the last couple centuries, and although the business itself is changing profoundly, their experience and capabilities are still extremely valuable. If you publish traditionally, you have a team to rely on, people who are experts in their fields. With self-publishing, there's a lot of "self" involved. That's why it's important for self-publishers to consider consulting with a team of people who are experts in their respected fields, to learn from them and to get their help in areas that are not your strengths. Just because we write a book doesn't mean we can do everything ourselves. Keep that in mind, because when you self-publish it's easy to be overcome with doubt when you have to create eBook files, design book covers, or do marketing. The good news is that you can hire people with those strengths to help you.

Why should you choose self-publishing? If you can't convince a traditional publisher to take the risk on your book, then you may be better off choosing self-publishing. However, there are other reasons to opt for self-publishing, such as to retain editorial and creative control, to get to the market quicker, to earn more royalties, to keep your book in print as long as you want, and to maintain full rights to your work.

Most of us want to be traditionally published. However, even if a traditional publisher publishes your book, it could take years before it's in print. Furthermore, being published does not automatically equal success. Your book must make back the investment the publisher puts into it, and if it doesn't, it could have a shorter shelf life than expected. Worse, if your book flops and the publisher decides to take it out of print, you might not have the rights to do anything further with your book. With self-publishing you have more time to gain a readership, and of course, you can update, modify, and market your book whenever you want because the rights remain solely yours.

After talking with others who have traditionally published, I discovered that my books have actually done better than some of theirs. Why? *I don't know for certain.* The best explanation I have come up with is: *connection* and the authentic relationships I have personally developed with my readers through my writing, my online platforms, and being a committed member of their communities. The Internet has provided a way to get your work out to readers without the help of deep pockets, and if you've done your job of connecting with your readers, your work can spread like never before. If it does spread, then you could be in a better position to negotiate if a traditional publisher becomes interested.

One Boy's Struggle was presented to a film producer, and although a film about my story has fallen through for the moment, if the book were to be made into a movie I would not need to share any royalties with a publisher. The rights to my book are entirely mine. That's a benefit to think about. If a traditional publisher decides to buy the rights to my book, and I accept the offer, then my royalties and rights would change.

So many wonderful things have happened in my writing life thanks to both writing and publishing *One Boy's Struggle*, but what if I had paid heed to that editor who said I can't publish it the way it was written? Or if I would have called it quits when I was rejected? I don't know, but I think it's a good thing I published on my own. Some might tell you that you shouldn't publish. I might tell you to publish, but should you really? Only you can decide that, no editor or even publisher, for that matter, can make that choice for you.

Self-Publishing is Easy

In this section, I'm going to give a basic introduction of Print-On-Demand publishing, the type of publishing I use. Print-On-Demand, or POD, simply means that a company can print copies of your book as the book is ordered rather than in huge, expensive printings with thousands of copies. Print-On-Demand is the reason why self-publishing has become so affordable. The company I chose, Infinity Publishing, made publishing my books trouble-free, and although they print hard copies, they also format and distribute electronic copies of my books via Amazon and many other online stores. (Note: I'm not endorsing or advertising for Infinity Publishing.)

Self-publishing a book isn't as complicated as you might expect. I researched many reputable self-publishing companies online and picked a highly rated one that offered what I wanted at the time in 2007. I provided them with my manuscript, paid them, and in a few months my book was available for sale on nearly every major bookseller's Website. When my book started selling, the publisher started sending me royalty checks. It was that simple.

The most complicated, time consuming part of the entire process wasn't self-publishing. That was easy compared to the actual writing of my book and getting the word out. Starting and finishing the writing is the part where most novices and even many experienced writers have the most difficulty, which is why this book's focus is on overcoming doubt. Still, I think a short introduction on the basics of self-publishing and blogging might be helpful to you as well, especially if you're new to publishing.

There's a lot to learn about self-publishing. Try not to let it overwhelm you because it doesn't need to. Having a good understanding of the basics gets most people by. The three most important things to look for in a company you're considering should be their quality, reputation and the actual services they provide. It is best to shop around, and find the best fit for you and your book's needs.

When researching self-publishing options, I soon realized there were many companies to choose from, so I narrowed my results to what would be easiest and most practical for me. I wanted a self-publisher that *offered a package that fit my needs.* All self-publishing companies offer various packages at different price ranges, starting with barebones publishing of paperback and digital editions, the next package might add copyediting, and more advanced packages may offer both copyediting and marketing. Packages and prices vary from company to company. I found several different companies that offered the services I wanted. I decided to look at price vs. royalties to find the one that would give me the best return on my investment. Then I researched their reputations by reading reviews and author experiences to find out which one was most reliable and reputable.

It's important to decide what you will need from a self-publishing company, and if you will have separate professionals help you with certain aspects of publishing your work. To save money you can do parts of it yourself, but if you want the best opportunity to appeal to a wide audience of readers I advise hiring professionals. Professionals really do make a difference in the creation of your book. I know I am hammering home the idea of hiring professionals, but only because it's that important. Keep in mind your book will be compared by readers to traditionally-published books, even if you're not directly competing with those books. This is part of the reason that self-publishing is frowned upon, because too many self-published authors skip the professional touches that could give their book the edge that it needs in order to be considered of high quality. Traditionally-published books normally have such standards without question. I am not saying you must use professionals, but I am saying that to an extent, regardless of how great your story is, you're dealing with perceptions from readers that you should strive to meet.

I do have some graphic design experience, so to save money I originally designed my own covers. But as I've revealed already, I decided to find a decent editor to help eliminate typos and edit for clarity. I suggest finding a professional book-cover designer, unless you have graphic design and marketing experience. Many self-publishers offer book cover designing and they likely offer it in one of their packages.

Be wary of how much you decide to spend on the whole self-publishing process. There are self-publishing options available for as low as a couple hundred dollars, and there are options available for thousands of dollars. But if you go digital only such as with Amazon's Kindle Direct Publishing as I have with my last few books, it's free (not including the costs you might have for any professionals you hire, of course).

One problem self-published authors run into is that they don't fully realize how long it takes to get the word out about their book. Some might not build any kind of readership for years. You may need to hire a reputable book marketing professional, but if you're on a budget like I was when I started, then you're probably going to need to do most of the marketing yourself. The bottom line here is that for most of us, we must carefully consider how much we're going to invest because there is the very real probability that we might not make the entire costs back through sales if we over invest. Evaluate how much you can afford and continue your research with that amount in mind.

In addition to the three major things I listed above, here are a few more details and considerations that may save you some time.

Self-Publishing Tips:

- Look for a reputable self-publishing company, one that has many satisfied authors to its credit already. If you're not sure their authors are satisfied, email a few of them to ask about their experience. It is usually easy to find their contact information. If the publisher has attached an online bookstore, there's usually a "contact the author" link. If not, then contact authors through their personal blogs. If you visit an author's blog, she may already be sharing information about her publishing experience, so check there first. A good sign that authors are satisfied with a company is if they have published several books with them.

- Use an online search engine to find reviews about any

self-publishing company you're interested in. Look for reviews that compare publishing services.

- What do you want to pay to publish your book? In my experience, pricing is extremely varied and does not always indicate the quality of the service you will actually receive. It's impossible to give you an estimate of what you might pay. There are very expensive to budget-friendly pricing, and several different types of packages. I made sure to find a publisher that had a price I could live with.

- Royalties, the amount of money you get from each book sold, vary between the publishers. I considered the cost to publish in relation to the royalty payments when making my choice. An important consideration is whether your readers can purchase directly from your publisher or if they can only purchase from a 3rd party online bookseller. If readers can purchase directly from your publisher you should earn more in royalties (paperback), but if your readers must purchase from a 3rd party site, like Amazon, then you could earn less. But that, of course, might not be the case if Amazon happens to be your publisher.

- If you want control of your book's design and layout, and even setting the retail price, then you want to make sure those are possible before making your choice.

- Make a list of any questions you have. When you have narrowed down the publishers you're interested in, then give them a phone call or send an email with your specific questions. This will also give you a good idea of their response time and customer service skills. But remember, there's no guarantee that a company's representatives have the same attitude after you have spent your money, so it's still important to check out their reviews.

- Check the "rights of the author" policy of any publisher

you're considering. I recommend retaining all of your rights. You should also have the option to leave the publisher when you're ready to move on, such as when a traditional publisher wants to publish your work. Read the contract thoroughly. It is a good idea to have a lawyer look over it. Also makes sure any formatting they do as part of their package is given to you for your records. For example if they make files for Kindle or other devices, make sure they give you copies of those files.

- The best self-publishing companies typically have all the information you need available on their websites. They should have a F.A.Q. which will cut your research time considerably. They may even have a free eBook to download that describes their services and various offerings.

- Books in eBook formats are becoming increasingly popular, so the best self-publishing companies should offer this as an option. Some of you may decide to *only* go digital, and find great success that way. If you're only going digital I recommend Amazon KDP. Your royalties for digital copies should be much higher than for print versions. There are offerings available at this time with upwards of 70% in royalties for digitally self-published books.

An important note about self-publishing: it's easy to do and it doesn't take much expertise. Because of this, it's easy to fail to give your book as much attention to detail as it deserves. The quality of books from many self-published authors is low, which gives self-publishing a bad reputation. This deserves to be repeated because it's too common a problem. However, for you and me, this is actually very good news since the authors who actually produce high quality books will be the cream that rises to the top. Make sure yours is the best it can be.

Even after becoming a bestselling author, I didn't quit my day job. My advice to anyone reading this is that you consider hanging on to your day job for a while longer. I don't want to discourage you from pursuing your passion to write full time. Far from it. Sometimes, though, we can get very excited about what we're doing and think everyone else will be as excited. Getting the word out about our books takes time, and there's no way to predict what the returns may be.

Try to have the long view in mind. In other words, write books that will be as relevant years from now as possible. Ask yourself if the information in your book will still be valuable five years from now. And be ready to allow the time it takes for your book to become known. Everyone's experience is different.

No matter how long it takes, keep writing. You never know—your first book may be the springboard for future books.

What I provided in this chapter is a basic overview and I recommend further reading, *APE: Author, Publisher, Entrepreneur—How to Publish a Book* by Guy Kawasaki and Shawn Welch. It's a great book that will give you the details you need to self-publish your work successfully. I interviewed Guy Kawasaki about *APE*, you can read it on Positive Writer, if you like. Another book you might want to consider is *Publishing E-Books For Dummies* by Ali Luke.

A free book chock full of useful information about getting published is *The Bestseller Labs Guide For Authors* by Jonathan Gunson. You can download a copy at Bestsellerlabs.com/the-bestseller-labs-guide-for-authors/ It's free, but you will be required to sign in with an email address to download it.

How to Promote Your Book in Online Communities

When a tree falls in the forest with no one around, does it make a noise?

Cliché, I know. But, it's a relevant question to any book author.

In this section, I want to give you a very basic overview about marketing online, mostly in communities. I did not originally plan on including marketing tips in this book, but I think some of my unique experiences—mostly lessons learned from marketing blunders—might help give you some ideas. Marketing your book online can be time consuming, but it's a requirement for any author who wants to see their books spread.

Lots of first time authors hap*hazardly* create blogs, Facebook pages, and comment on any and every article that has anything remotely to do with their subject matter. Yes, that will sell a few books. However, don't do these things without full consideration of what and why you're doing them. Instead, design a plan to clearly identify what your book is about and who it will best serve. Your audience may widen later, as happened with *One Boy's Struggle*, but first you want to start small and get to know your specific audience.

Once you realize what group of people your book will best serve, then you'll want to get to know that group by visiting their online hangouts. These are easy to discover by doing an online search with the key word for your niche and adding the keywords "community," "forums," or "social network." Then find out what's already being done to serve the community and who's doing it. Get to know them and become a *valuable* contributor. But whatever you do, try not to come across as desperate for people to buy your book. Let them get to know you. If you try to announce your book in every comment and forum thread, eventually they might kick you out of their conversations or ignore you. Thousands of book authors have tried to do that and communities are weary of it. You don't want to turn off any community by being overzealous. It's best to keep your book on the "down low" until the community accepts you as a contributor. Even when they do accept you, still avoid over-broadcasting your book. What you really want is to become a known contributor to the community. As people get to know you in online communities and trust you, they'll be interested in visiting your website and interacting with you. In other words, book marketing begins with building relationships.

These points are mostly for use in online communities, but the basic principles can apply other places as well:

- Be a regular contributor to any community, network or group you join. Be selective, because if you join too many you may not be able to valuably contribute to all of them. Community members normally want to be able to count on you, that you will reply or provide further information.

- If you join a forum or blog post on a community site, bookmark it to return to later or create email notifications so that you will be alerted to replies. Whenever someone makes a comment try your best to respond and keep the conversations going.

- If you join a community in order for people to visit your webpage, contribute valuable content regularly and become known as helpful, respectful and available. By doing that community members may want to get to know you better and spread the word about how helpful and sincere you are. They need a reason to spread your good name, so do your best to give it to them.

- It is quite common for bloggers to repost their blog posts to several communities across the internet. If you do this, just remember to bookmark those places so that you can contribute to any conversations they create.

- Comment on other people's forums and blog posts. You don't want to come across as if it's all about you, commenting and active participation will help you avoid such an erroneous perception.

- Try not to argue and debate too much online. Even if you're right, doing these things may potentially cast a negative light on you. Internet forums have become well known for "flame wars," great argument matches between members, and lots of people have come to resent such activity, with good reason. Those who participate in such commotions are generally not well regarded. You will get attention, for sure, but not all attention is good. With that in mind, consider that anything you post online in public forums could last forever.

- Feedback is your ally. Let community members and your readers know that you value comments and recommendations, that you're willing to listen and consider their viewpoints. If you show you genuinely care and express that in the form of your responses, you're highly likely to generate honesty and loyalty, all the while offering your loyalty to them as well.

- In the communities you join, if there isn't already a private messaging system, provide a way for members to contact you. You can contact me at Bryan.Hutchinson (at) positivewriter.com. I use the (at) to replace @ so online spam bots to don't discover and use the email address.

- Give your best effort to answer your readers' emails to you. My advice is never use a "standard" reply. Standard replies tend to create distance and may disconnect you from your readers. Try not to use "out of office" or "I'll get back to you, but I am too busy" replies. You're not a conglomerate. You're a real person and readers want to know that. Such replies are sometimes interpreted as: "I am too good to answer this right away!" Also, with regard to emails, try not to employ a system that requires the people who send you email to prove their email isn't spam. Again, it creates distance and could suggest arrogance on your part. Instead, take the time to check your spam folder once a week. In other words, don't make potential readers do extra work to contact you.

- If by chance you write for a specific niche and cannot find an online network dedicated to it, then consider creating one (if you have the time, the funds, and can dedicate yourself). This was the case in my niche. I created one of the first social networks within my niche and it has grown to thousands of members. I consider it the highlight of all that I have done, even more so than writing my books, because I have met so many courageous people and developed life-long relationships that I otherwise might not have. Our network continues to grow everyday and although I admit I can't always keep up with it as much as I would like, I do my very best.

Why You Need a Blog and to Giveaway Free eBooks

Do you want to build your audience and develop relationship with readers? Two effective ways are to post frequently on your blog and give away eBooks for free.

Since we've been talking about online communities, a great way to become known as a contributor is to blog, writing articles that pertain to your community. On your blog you can display your book covers and short descriptions, but to attract people to your blog you will need to write content that will fascinate your readers and keep them coming back. One of the best ways to write such valuable content is to tell your story in articles, openly sharing your life-lessons for free and commenting insightfully on the latest happenings in your community. It is easier to attract readers to your blog than to your book, since it's free and simple to access. As you become more accepted and known in your online communities you can ask fellow bloggers to link to your blog and likewise link back to them, building your ranking with search engines and becoming known to other audiences. Communities, rather than strangers, are far more open to being asked to visit a blog. After all, blogs are a part of the online information highway. Of course, just as you don't want to over-promote your book in your communities, you don't want to over-promote your blog, either. If you've gotten to know the members of your community, then you should be building lasting relationships with fellow bloggers and helping each other spread the word about each other's blogs.

In today's online market, the key is to help each other, fellow writers, fellow bloggers and our readers. This is how community works best. The old days of competition between us are gone, and those who still hold on to the old competitive ways are finding themselves abandoned. You don't want to be alone.

There is a difference between a blog and a static website that only has your name and information on it along with a few pictures of your books. I mention this because there's sometimes confusion between the two. Every author starting out in self-publishing should have a frequently updated blog. A static page is hard to find and gives very little incentive to a reader to come back to it. A blog, on the other hand, is alive as an online, public journal with new information that you post regularly. That's what avid readers want from authors.

Why blog? Here are several reasons:

- To have an online journal of your writing where readers can find and interact with you.
- To gain readership in your area of knowledge or experience.
- To be viewed as an expert in your field.
- To advertise your books by attracting readers to your free content (e.g. blog posts, free eBooks). *Note: A good place to advertise your books is in your sidebar.*
- To have fun with your writing.
- To contribute to your community and connect with others.
- To practice writing and publishing.
- To say and share something important.
- To write a book, or publish parts of your book, to see how readers react to it.
- Because it's fun!

There are many tools and websites that allow you to blog for free. There are so many that it's best to do an online search. Just search for "blogging platforms" for several comprehensive lists. So far I have used Wordpress, and I like it, but I use it under my own domain (i.e. www.positivewriter.com). If you choose to use your own domain, then you will need to pay fees: the cost of a domain name, the cost from the host of the Website, (which basically means renting online space). Having your own website also means you will have to maintain it, which may be confusing or time consuming, especially if you're not technologically savvy.

A great book to read to learn detailed information about blogging is: *Blogging All-in-One for Dummies* by Susan Gunelius.

Once you have chosen your blogging platform, you're ready to write and tell the world your stories. Keep in mind that when you do publish something it's available to the world, so you will want to publish responsibly and keep within the law.

The reason I have been successful getting the word out about my books isn't only because of my blog. My success in getting the word out is really all about *my readers* who spread the word about my writing better than I ever could by myself. But how did I get readers, anyway? Well, it did start with my blog, but much of the success has come through sharing my experiences in several free eBooks. A couple of my free eBooks are very short, but I have also written full-length books and given them away for free when I could have sold them.

Most people appreciate generosity. I know many authors who worry about people simply taking their work without a second thought, but that's normal and why the eBooks are free to begin with. Yes, there are those who will take without as much as a thank you. I won't try and convince you otherwise. But you would be surprised by the number of people who read something of yours that was free and then are kind enough to share your work with others. When people share your work, it can in turn compel them and others to read more of your writing, specifically the book you're selling.

Once your free eBooks are out, nothing can stop them, nothing and no one. They are out there and if people enjoy them and connect with them, they will share them very far and wide, indeed. You'll never completely know how far your free eBooks will spread, because many readers attach the file to their emails to send to friends. Others upload them to sharing networks like Peer-to-Peer and Usenet.

My free eBooks have become so popular that bootleggers have uploaded them to sell them to take advantage of their popularity. I guess the positive side is that you know you're gaining recognition when the bootleggers notice you and try to take advantage. Bootleggers can be very good at spotting what readers will want to read. I share this with you so that you won't be wary of giving full books out for free. As a matter of fact, if you don't, you may have a very long road ahead of you because as more and more authors do this it's possible it will eventually become expected. If bootleggers do upload your book to Amazon or other sites to sell it, don't worry, I've been able to get Amazon and even B&N to remove bootlegged copies.

In today's market dominated by social media, many readers want to check out our writing *before* they buy from us, and a blog alone won't always cut it. The key is to get your readers to spread the word, and free eBooks make it very easy for readers by giving them something valuable they can share. Sample chapters of your book are good but are not shared as frequently as complete eBooks. It's very easy to create a free eBook. Simply write a short story or offer helpful tips in your niche, and convert to PDF, then upload it to your blog and offer it as a free download. Be sure to include links to your blog and your book page in the free eBook. If you're building an email list, then ask your existing readers to sign up to download it. Sharing your work this way can be technically challenging. I had some difficulty getting the hang of it, and I even had help. The good news is that there is an abundance of information online on how to create a free eBook and give it away. If you do an online search, you'll find all the instructions you need, and maybe find someone who can help you with the technical aspects at a low cost.

Trust your readers, as they know best how to get the word out. *All they have to do is like your writing and share it with their friends.* Gaining a readership is about exposing readers to your writing and then connecting with them. Blogs and free eBooks help us do that.

How do you use your blog to grow your readership? Tips:

- What is your blog about? Do you write in a specific niche? Know what topic you're going to write about the most and try to stick to it. If you've written a book and want to use your blog to help get the word out, write about the same subject as your book.

- Blog about what you know. It's easy, fun and rewarding. Even better, blog to help other readers learn new things about what you know. Offer tips and suggestions that have helped you firsthand. Everyone wants to learn, and bloggers who offer helpful advice usually attract the most readers. Therefore, share your experience and life-lessons. Avoid discounting your experience because what you believe won't be helpful to anyone could wind up being extremely helpful to many.

- Try to be consistent and persistent. If you can't blog every day, at least blog as often as possible. If your blog becomes stagnant for too long, readers may stop visiting your site.

- Be honest. Blog from the heart and say what you mean without trying to guess what people want to read. If you're always trying to say what others want you to say, you're likely not being honest with yourself or your readers. At the same time, you do want to try to meet your readers' expectations with what you have already consistently written about. It is okay to go off topic from time to time, but your reader base will expect to read about certain topics on your blog.

- Be encouraging. Everyone wants to be encouraged, including me (and probably you, too)!

- Comment on similar blogs that share your interests. Readers are attracted to people who build on the conversation and will likely want to read more of what you have to say.

- Create meaning. Stand for something and become a spokesperson.

- Write about your failures because you're human with real life issues.

- Write about your successes for the same reason.

- Use calls to action by asking questions of your readers, usually near the end of the blog post. Doing these things helps compel readers to comment and creates conversation.

- Don't worry if you don't get many comments. There are so many blogs on the Web that readers have very little time to comment on all the blogs that they visit. That doesn't mean they are not reading or that they don't care. If you live for comments, you may give up too early and not give yourself the chance to build a readership. However, you will find blogs with an overwhelming number of comments and this is often because their email list and popularity is very high. Just as in day-to-day life we do not compare ourselves to the A – list movies stars, we should not compare ourselves to A – list bloggers. With that said, on the internet the playing field is more even and you can build a readership that engages in the comments over time.

- Build your email list (email subscribers to your blog). This is very important. Not only does building your subscriber base help keep your readers up to date, but it will also increase the number of comments on your posts by reaching the people who are already interested in what you write about.

- When readers leave comments on your blog, respond to them. It's polite, builds conversations and gives readers a good reason to come back.

- Use comments and emails from readers to help you find new ideas to write about on your main topic(s). If a reader asks a question via your comment section or via email, and it's something a lot of people might be wondering about, try to write a blog post answering that question. I recommend not identifying the person who asked the question unless they give you permission to do so.

- Write about current issues that relate to your blog's main topic.

- Be mindful of the mood in which you blog. Few bloggers realize they convey their mood and attitude to their readers. If you blog in a pleasant, positive and helpful manner, then that is the mood you pass along to your readers. The same is true if you blog in an angry and negative manner. Which mood do you want to convey?

- Try to build relationships with other bloggers, perhaps by linking to their blogs through your own or helping them get the word out about certain events and goings on that they are promoting. They may help you do the same.

- Guest blog! Blogging is time consuming and many bloggers don't have the time to do it regularly. Offer to write free articles for other bloggers in your niche as a guest blogger. Guest blogging both helps you build relationships with fellow bloggers by providing them valuable content and it increases your exposure to new readers. Contacting bloggers is easy. Simply visit their blogs and find the "contact" button or comment on one of their blog posts. It helps to already have your blog up and running with articles posted so that they can see a sample of your writing and decide if it fits their blog's focus and would interest their audience.

- Blogging doesn't mean you have to please everyone, especially those who purposely disagree with everything you write. My blog is for like-minded individuals, and I don't have time or the need to try to please those who only want to rage or are overly critical. If you try to please everyone, an impossible task, you may burn out quickly.

- Remember, the most important part of your blog is content, as much content as you can generate. But not just any content will grow your readership. The more helpful, unique and interesting your blog posts are, the more readers you will attract and retain.

- If your blog is on your own domain, make sure you use the email address that comes with it. The email address also helps spread the word about your website. My email ends with @positivewriter.com which is my domain name and web address.

- Add a signature to your emails with your blog address. People forward emails all the time and is another way of getting the word out.

- There are many blog-indexing sites on the Internet. List your blog on as many as possible. Some bloggers and major websites list links to blogs that relate to their content. Submit your blog for those lists as well. When submitting, consider if your blog relates, because if it doesn't, then it may be rejected.

- Research legal issues, such as libel and posting copyrighted material.

- Have fun! If you enjoy what you're writing about, then it's likely others will enjoy it, too.

How do you market your book online through your blog? Tips:

- Share excerpts of your book as blog posts. This is a great way to start letting your audience know about your forthcoming book. It's also a good way to test potential interest. If you're a regular reader of my blog Positive Writer, you may have noticed a few familiar passages from this book, that's because I've posted slightly modified excerpts in the form of blog posts to see how readers would respond to the content. It helps to know when you're connecting and it's also good to know when you're not.

- Create PDF's of sample chapters of your book to share on your blog or other websites. PDF's are easy to attach to emails so this makes it very convenient for your readers to download and share them. To make sure your PDF files are shareable, make the file size as small as possible. You can use a program like PDF Shrinker to reduce these files. (Here's a free online tool: http://compress-pdf.co.uk/).

- Use your blog to review books by other authors, and if the author is interested, to give away signed copies of those books. You can do this by announcing to your readers that after a specific date you will randomly draw one of their names from the comment section. After they comment, you can then put their names in a hat and draw one of them. Whenever an author asks you to review his or her book, simply ask them if they would like to provide signed copies to give away. You'll need a copy of the book to review anyway, and I have rarely met an author who turns this down.

- If you write a blog post about a certain subject that was also in your book, try to incorporate your book's title into the post.

- Make it easy for readers to subscribe to your blog by putting an email signup form at the top of your sidebar.

- Make it easy for readers to share your blog's content via social networking sites and emailing. Most blogging platforms have great plug-ins that make this simple.

- Every now and then, give *your* book away as a free prize to readers who frequently comment. Create a contest out of it.

- Invite readers to review your book on major book selling sites, especially Amazon. If they do, ask them if you can use their reviews as testimonials. There are services available to help you get reviews, such as Story Cartel which helped me get over 100 honest reviews in exchange for a free copy of my book *Happy Every Day—Simple, Effective Ways to Better Days*. For more details on how I got so many reviews read this: http://positivewriter.com/how-i-got-over-100-

reviews-on-amazon-in-less-than-3-weeks/

- Ask well-known authors in your niche to read your book and offer testimonials and endorsements. Post those testimonials on your blog.

- Offer to participate in interviews with bloggers in your niche. Participate in podcast or radio interviews. Don't wait for people to ask you. Feel free to seek out bloggers, podcasters or radio stations and offer to do interviews. Ask if you can have a digital copy so you can post it on your blog after it airs.

- Create short videos discussing the topics you write about or offer "how to" instructional videos. Post them to your blog and allow them to easily be shared with other sites.

- Consider doing podcasts. This is similar to writing blog articles, but instead you're creating audio versions. It's also a great way to do shout-outs to the frequent commenters on your blog and answer any questions they may have posted in comments or emailed to you. Let your readers know about podcasts ahead of time and ask them to send you questions.

There are endless possibilities to market your book online and I've only scratched the surface. By far, maintaining a blog and sharing free eBooks has helped me the most. It took a lot of time and dedication to get the word out. I thought my book would spread much more rapidly. A lot of writers have great expectations when they start, but to see those expectations come true, you'll have to stick with it. Days may turn into months and months may turn into years, but if you follow through, you'll come to a point when you know your strategies are working. As I've made clear, there are no guarantees and you may be able to find quicker ways than I did. For example, if you can get on TV or radio to give interviews, that will help. Also, if you speak at seminars, make sure to have copies of your book with you, or at least business cards to hand out with the title of your book and your blog address on it.

I'm a huge advocate of making free content available for sharing. Having free content that your readers can share makes the job of getting the word out much simpler, smoother and, most importantly, less imposing. Additionally, free content benefits your readers. My current top downloaded and shared free eBook has about 100,000 downloads that I know of and I have no idea how many times it has been shared via email or sharing sites, so at a minimum that's 100,000 people who have sampled my writing! Not to mention the other free eBooks I have available, with thousands of downloads among them as well. At the end of each free eBook I placed pictures, reviews and links to my print books and to my websites.

My free eBooks will continue to spread and that's publicity that can't be purchased for any price. It's authentic, generous and readers don't feel obligated to buy anything. Besides, it also shows your readers that you're not just in it for the money, and hopefully that's true. Still, you have to eat like everyone else. Instead, you can consider these eBooks as free samples. However, if you create free eBooks be sure to make them as complete and remarkable as possible or the effort may not accomplish anything. My first free eBooks were poorly designed, but for the latest one, I hired a professional designer to create the cover for me. What a major difference and impact that has made. I highly recommend adding a professional's touch to your free work when you can, to improve the presentation. Today's readers may be more interested in content and connection, but they do still appreciate quality.

There are thousands of good strategy suggestions online on how to market your book. I highly suggest researching them, but doing all of them isn't always needed or even recommended. Consider starting with the easiest, most basic tips first and progressing slowly. Take your time and try to be patient as word about your book spreads. Doing this will help prevent you from trying to do too much and stretching yourself too thin. Most of us want to create something viral, but sometimes going viral happens when you're patient and focused on constantly creating quality content. Eventually you may create something (a free eBook, video, podcast or blog post) that suddenly spreads like wildfire. Trust me, if creating something viral were easy, everyone would be doing it. You never know for certain what will work until it does. I expected my free eBooks to be downloaded perhaps a few hundred times, I had no idea any of them would go viral and be downloaded over a hundred thousand times.

In addition to seeking out marketing plans online, consider visiting author forums and social networks, too. There are many websites where new writers, as well as veterans of the craft, communicate and share ideas, experiences and opinions. There's a vast amount of information available, but like everything else take your time and read first what pertains to you. After a while you will probably be the one sharing your marketing and writing advice.

There's something you will want to try to avoid when marketing your book and that is over the top, "in-your-face" marketing strategies. Yes, you need to get the word out about your book if you want people to discover it, but a lot of people are wary of being marketed to online. As I've pointed out, people like to discover things and to learn about new stuff through trusted friends and word of mouth. An author's word that his or her book is the best thing ever written is less convincing than a trusted friend telling you the same thing. Of course, readers know you have to market your book. It's when you overdo it that it may come across the wrong way and become a turn-off. Marketing is extremely important and, when done respectfully, can be well received and beneficial for both you and your readers.

Over-the-top marketing tactics to avoid:

- Popup advertising is usually perceived as an annoyance. Try not to force popup advertising on your blog readers. If you do, make it easy to disable so visitors don't give up and leave your page.

- "Sign up for this" in order to read content on your website. It's a good idea to ask visitors to sign up to your email list to download your free eBooks or other special content, but try to avoid making it a condition to read what's on your website. Whenever I visit a site that requires me to sign up for something before I can actually read any content on the site, I tend to click the close box and leave. I advise making your website easy to access without any "sign up" system that could be perceived as an annoyance. If your website is valuable to the visitor, then they'll choose to sign up to download your special content or to participate in discussions on their own. You don't need to force their hand.

- Making all of your blog posts, social media posts, and online conversations about your book. This gets old fast. It's better to find out what people are talking about in your niche and join the conversation. Let people get to know you without being bombarded about your book. The more people get to know you, the more likely they may want to read your work.

- Many of the strategies available online are what's called "interrupt marketing." Before using a new strategy, ask yourself if you would like to experience it if *you* were a visitor or reader. Do you want to be interrupted? For further information on such marketing and how to use the opposite, which is called "Permission Marketing" visit Seth Godin's excellent blog: sethgodin.typepad.com.

- *Normally $100,000 worth of information for a limited time for $1.00!* Doesn't an ad like that send out a warning signal? I think discounts are great, but if they come across as unrealistic then that may also make your entire efforts seem less than authentic.

- The key for me has been to consider what type of impression I am giving. If I am perceived as trying to make a quick buck, I will fail at being a respected part of the community. That's the problem with some of the "quick-buck marketing strategies," they make your efforts seem less worthy than they truly are. I am not saying you can't use those strategies, or that they are absolutely "wrong," but just consider the perception they may create about you.

- Avoid being rash, such as spamming potential readers with offers to buy your book. If there's one thing I know for certain is that if we respect our readership and are as generous as possible with them, they will be more apt to support us in return. I can't emphasize this enough. My books and online efforts first and foremost grew out of the desire to be of service to others and to provide them with resources. I am extremely fortunate to have a readership of individuals who are not only wonderful, positive people, who are informative and fun to interact with, but who are also generous in supporting my efforts and spreading the word about my work. I really don't think I would have gotten to this level by doing anything thoughtlessly.

Consider reading *Sell Your Book Like Wildfire—The Writer's Guide To Marketing & Publicity* by Rob Eagar.

Why You Should Dream Big

It's cliché to say dream big, and many of us stop ourselves from doing it with the knowledge that it must be realistic. Dreaming big in today's world is akin to asking for trouble. Many of us have been indirectly (and directly) taught to think realistically, to not have dreams and aspirations beyond our personal circumstances. Writing and publishing a book is for the elite, don't you agree?

I hope you don't buy into "realistic thinking," or that writing and publishing is only for the elite. I included my personal history in this book to demonstrate that having a dream isn't farfetched. You should not give up on it because you don't meet someone else's standards. I wrote this book with the aspiration to help others on their writing journey. I've even included a few tips on how to publish and get the word out about your work. Many have written books about writing before me, great writers, in fact. I mean, seriously, who do I think I am? That question alone could have filled me with overwhelming doubt (it did) and stopped me from writing this book (it didn't). Experts have told me to give up on my dream, sending me the message loud and clear that I am not good enough. If I were thinking realistically, I should never have written this book, right?

If you have been told you're not good enough, should you simply give up and not aspire to live your dream? People have been succeeding for ages in areas in which they were told that they would never make it. Sometimes you have to dream big anyway.

Dream the biggest dream you can, and, at the same time, make your dream doable. "Dreamers," I think, are mistakenly labeled as those who dream about something but do nothing to actually go out and bring their dream into reality. Dreamers who do not try to find practical ways to make their dreams a reality should more aptly be named "wishers." "Wishers" expect their dreams to just happen for them without any effort on their part. My advice is to not become a "wisher," and instead, to find the ways that you can "do" what you dream. Be a dreamer, and be certain that you're not merely wishing! Wishing isn't a bad thing, we all have our wishes, but it's important to know the difference.

To start turning your dream into a reality, answer these questions:

- What is your dream?
- How can you accomplish your dream?
- What specific steps do you need to take?
- What do you need as far as the necessary tools?
- Who can help you?

Those are very important questions. What if you didn't need anyone's approval? What if you could just go out and work to accomplish your heart's desires? What if you didn't have any doubts? Set yourself free to take the necessary steps required to do what you want to do. "Wishers" tend to hope someone will do it for them, or that it will somehow fall into their lap. But dreamers have a vision. They take the time to identify that vision and the steps necessary to achieve it. Then they start working toward that dream, often with the right people who can help them.

Dream big, as big and grand as you want to! Then take a few moments and explain in writing (for yourself) how you're going to go out and get it. Having a plan is the key to actually achieving. No matter how grand a dream may be, it doesn't need to be farfetched or out of your reach if you develop and follow a plan. Dreams are only out of reach if we wait for them to come to us and don't go out and intentionally do what is necessary to turn them into reality.

You don't have to have all the answers. It is the act of starting that helps us discover the answers and direction we need. If you want to publish a book, then first start writing. As the book develops, research what you'll need to do next. Create a short list of steps you will take. A plan does not have to be an impressive outline of details right away, but rather a list of specific overall basic steps. Such as:

- Write
- Publish
- Market

The list is basic, but extremely useful because it's what you're actually going to do. As you continue on your journey and learn new things that you need to do, fill in details between each step, creating a general summary of your plan, something like this:

- Write
    - What's the story about?
    - Approximately how many pages will it be?
    - Who will edit it?
- Publish
    - Seek an agent or publisher?
    - Self-publish: Which company to use?
    - Make available in print or as an eBook, or both?
- Market
    - Discover, join and become involved in communities about the book's subject.
    - Create a blog.
    - Create a press release.

K.I.S.S. — Keep It Simple and Straightforward. A plan doesn't need to be over the top with details. It only needs to give you direction when you're not sure of what you should do next. My preference is to use questions in my list of steps but each step could be a statement instead. Questions compel me to do more research and discover more about what I can do. Even so, it's still very important to remember that ultimately *I am a writer*, and not get lost in so many details that I get brain locked. It is possible to create a list of steps that is too detailed and too long, so that the whole project becomes overwhelming. Try not to fall into that trap. Use the K.I.S.S. method. The simpler the better, because the more complex it gets the more likely Writer's Doubt may stop you.

How to become a Professional Author

Let's be honest with each other, you and I both know how doubt about yourself and your abilities can tear you apart. I wasted too many years living with overwhelming doubt. It's a painful struggle that we all endure and must overcome. We don't become true professionals until we have slain the beast within. It's a rite of passage. It's a psychological conflict because most writers are ashamed of their own uncertainty. Instead of slaying the beast, many of us label ourselves as "starving artists," which is a way of justifying the lack of recognition we've received. We believe that if we're recognized for our writing then we will feel validated. But therein is yet another conundrum: *Recognition*.

Want-to-be-professional writers too often believe they need to achieve some kind of milestone to officially call themselves professional. The milestone might be selling their work, being tagged by a recognized expert in their field, writing their first book, or publishing it. But there's a problem with milestones, and I'm sure you already know this problem well. No matter how many milestones you reach, it will never be enough.

True professionals don't need milestones. Professionals are professionals because they have overcome, and continue to overcome, Writer's Doubt. They're professionals because they're doing work that matters every day in spite of their internal and external critics. They wake up, sharpen their pencils and write.

Doubt still exists within the professional, but it does not rule. A professional does the work, writes the story that needs to be written, and goes to bed knowing he or she will get up the next morning and continue. A professional does not need to tell herself she is a professional, because she knows that being a professional is the action of working and publishing. It's a result, and results matter. The more she works, the more she publishes. And as a result she is hired for more work. When her work is rejected she gets back to writing and does what needs to be done to improve.

If you strive every day to do work that matters and submit it for publication, regardless if it's accepted or rejected, then you're a professional writer. It's not overly complicated, so don't let your doubt over complicate it.

Consider a professional in your field. Anyone will do. Now let me ask you, does that person need to tell you he or she is a professional? Then why would you need to tell yourself that you're a professional? If you do the work and ship, then you're a professional. Once you accept this simple truth your name will become synonymous with professionalism, and you'll never need to tell yourself or anyone else you're a professional again.

> **"When I was a child my mother said to me, 'If you become a soldier, you'll be a general. If you become a monk, you'll be the pope.' Instead I became a painter and wound up as Picasso."**
>
> —Pablo Picasso

Create Work That Matters

Congratulations! You've just about finished a unique book. It's probably not entirely what you expected, and that's why I wrote it.

If you still feel dazed and confused anywhere during the process of writing and find yourself back in a tunnel of darkness, that's okay, put your hands against the wall and lead yourself forward until you see in the distance a glimmer of light, go towards it by *writing*.

As writers, we have the tendency to feel things deeply, and therefore we often dread what we write as much as we love it. It's from our passion, I believe, that we agonize so much about critics, rejection, and our own personal angst. Whether you think you're making sense or not, whether you think others will care or not, and whether anyone will read what you write or not, write anyway. Write with purpose, because only when you put pen to paper and write can you overcome Writer's Doubt and create work that matters.

You, my friend, are remarkable, and you are a writer. If you want to be a remarkable writer, there's one thing you absolutely must do, and that is be you. Most people try so hard to be what they think others want them to be and only write things they think others want to read. That's not writing. That's frustrating, and it's fake. Just be yourself. You are a very interesting writer, with a unique voice, and I'm sure you have a compelling story to share, so don't hide it.

We need your story. Write it, because *that's* what writer's do. You have the Audacity to be a writer. And that's a good thing.

~*Bryan Hutchinson*

PS: If you enjoyed this book, do me a small favor, help spread the word about it on Facebook, Twitter and any other social networks where you hang out. Thank you! And don't forget to connect with me at http://positivewriter.com.

Resources

Throughout this book I have mentioned several resources you may find helpful. If you'd like a list of those resources I've created an online page for quick reference: http://positivewriter.com/writing-resources/

Free Book

For access to download your free eBook, "Good Enough – Stop Seeking Perfection and Approval," go to this web link: http://positivewriter.com/free-ebook-good-enough/

Or simply go to **www.PositiveWriter.com** and click on the Free Book link in the menu.

About The Author

Bryan Hutchinson is a renowned author of several bestselling books and an award winning blogger. He's sometimes humorous and sometimes serious, but he's always insightful, positive, and enthusiastic. Bryan spends his spare time visiting historic locations with his wife, Joan Faith.

Made in the USA
San Bernardino, CA
01 October 2017